# A Youthful Spirit

# *A Youthful Spirit*

Edited by

Pete Ward and Lindsay Urwin OGS

© Tufton Books
Faith House
7 Tufton Street
London SW1P 3QN

Tufton Books is a publishing imprint of the Church Union

First published in 1998

ISBN 0-85191-233-8

Typeset by Phoenix Photosetting, Chatham, Kent
Printed in Great Britain by
Redwood Books, Trowbridge, Wilts

# Contents

# Contributors

**Dean Borgman** is an Episcopal Priest, and Culpepper Professor of Youth Ministry at Gordon Conwell Seminary, USA

**Patrick Butler** works for the Anglican Church, developing youth ministry in the diocese of Paraguay, South America

**Emily Choge** is a lecturer in the Department of Religion at Moi University, Kenya

**Sheryl A. Kujawa** is Associate Professor of pastoral theology and Director of congregational studies at the Episcopal Divinity School, Cambridge, Massachusetts, USA

**David Moxon** is the Bishop of Waikato, New Zealand

**Yazeed Said** is an ordinand from the diocese of Jerusalem, studying at Westcott House, Cambridge

**Thomas Smith** is a school chaplain in Sydney, Australia

**Lindsay Urwin OGS** is Bishop of Horsham in the UK

**Pete Ward** is the Archbishop of Canterbury's Adviser for Youth Ministry, and research fellow at King's College, London

**Helen Wilderspin** is the National Tikanga Pakeha Youth Facilitator for New Zealand

# Foreword

Amongst many other things the Lambeth Conference of 1998 provided me with was a series of wonderful encounters and deeply enriching experiences. One of those – and this is something which I hope I shall never forget – was the dynamism of the Eagles Wings Cheerleaders as they swept into the main Conference Hall with all the energy and enthusiasm that young people are capable of showing.

For me that session, which they contributed to, was one of the highlights of the Conference. In retrospect it enabled many Bishops to recapture something of their vision for the work the Church can do with young people – and the difference young people can make to the Church. This book, co-authored by two of those who planned that session, breathes the life of that 'Youthful Spirit' which reinvigorated us all. It is a volume which I hope that those responsible for the life of the Church will read, and then apply to their own situations. It presents stories from a wide variety of cultural and ecclesiastical backgrounds, but there are plenty of lessons for all of us to learn from it.

I am grateful to Pete Ward, Lindsay Urwin and to all its contributors and I warmly commend it to you.

+George Cantuar

Archbishop of Canterbury

# Introduction

Young people are right at the heart of the Church's life, or at least they should be. At the recent Lambeth Conference ministry amongst children and young people was identified as one of the key priorities of the Anglican Church over the coming years. At the Conference a presentation entitled *A Youthful Spirit* offered a glimpse of life and energy of the young people in the Church, and insights into the challenges we face in mission to those outside.

This book, which goes by the same title as the youth presentation, offers more extensive reflections on youth ministry by many of those involved in the original presentation. These include Bishops Moxon and Urwin, Professor Dean Borgman, Pete Ward and Yazeed Said. Their writing, and the other material in this book, offer an insight into the exciting range and style of ministry amongst young people across the Anglican Communion. The message is one of hope and optimism. Much good work is already being done, but we all recognize that the task before us is very great.

As Jesus took the children upon his knee, he taught his disciples the importance of young people in the things of the Kingdom. Young people are not a problem to be solved, rather a sign of God's activity in our midst. The subculture, music and style of youth may leave the Church feeling a little behind the times, but at heart it is out of the life and energy of young people that the Church will find renewal. The Spirit of God is ever youthful and our Church must learn to catch the wind.

At the Lambeth Conference the Anglican Church recognized the importance of young people for the Church, but it also confessed the way that the adult world has created children of war, abused children and children who are victims of advertising. In a resolution passed by the bishops (Resolution II.8), the Lambeth Conference:

(a) recognises and celebrates the dynamic work of God among young people, and their infinite value in the human family. They are for us in the Church, as they were for Jesus, signs of the Kingdom of God among us. Their presence and ministry in the church is essential for the whole family of God to be complete. As adults, we confess with deep humility and sorrow that the adult world has created children of war, children abused by neglect and sexual exploitation, and children who are victims of aggressive advertising. In joyful obedience to God we reaffirm our apostolic commitment to all young people everywhere;

(b) recognises the faithful and creative work by many church members in ministry with children both within and beyond the church's borders;

(c) resolves, for the health and welfare of the whole Church:

    (i) that the bishops of the Anglican Communion will commit themselves, and will give leadership in their dioceses, to ensure that the church is a safe, healthy, and spiritually enriching community for children and young people;

    (ii) that the bishops will give more attention to the furtherance of ministry to children as a recognition of their importance to God and as a foundation for all future ministry;

    (iii) that the bishops will commit themselves to give significant time over the next twelve months to meet with young people in their dioceses, listening to them, praying with them, searching the Scriptures and breaking bread together with them, and providing ways for them to be trained in leadership skills and to exercise that leadership in the life and mission of the Church;

    (iv) that such meetings should open out into attempts to meet and hear young people who have not yet been touched by the Gospel;

    (v) that teams of adults and young people in as many congregations as possible be trained for holistic ministry to young people outside the Church, so as to speak of God's love in Christ in ways that can be heard, and that Christian young people be equipped, in the power of the Holy Spirit, for service in Church and Community;

(vi)  that young people should be helped to find or maintain their spiritual home in the Anglican Church, where necessary by giving particular attention to matters of liturgy including the use of music and silences; and

(vii)  that urgent consideration be given to how best international Anglican networks of young people may be strengthened and serviced by the structures of the Communion.

These are challenging times for the Church as it reaches out to young people around the world. The Lambeth Conference gave a powerful sign that the Church is resolved to take on this challenge in a variety of ways. I welcome this book as an indication of a new direction for the Communion. A gospel commitment to young people. The chapters offer ways forward for all of us.

# 1

# Listening to Young People

## *Pete Ward*

The Church should listen to young people. Well, so the message normally goes – but why should we? What is so special about young people? Clergy, bishops and Church committees are surrounded by groups who are convinced that they have a particular right to be heard: older people, minority racial groups, those who fill the collections plates, women, children, homosexuals. And then there are the global voices of the poor and dispossessed. Everyone, seemingly, has a claim on the Church's attention. So why listen to young people?

Theological discourse has been characterized by two main approaches to listening to young people. A familiar line of argument would be that young people, as part of the Church, have a 'right' to be included. This is a matter of basic 'justice' which the Christian Gospel demands as an imperative. Young people, according to this approach, are marginalized and disadvantaged economically, socially and ecclesiastically. The Church is compelled by the Gospel to act in these three spheres to bring about God's Kingdom's rule. In essence this is the approach taken by Sheryl Kujawa in her discussion of 'Youth Ministry and Justice'. Discussion of inclusion and 'rights' connects to the institutional power of the Church to deny or to recognize the self-evident claims of young people. Driving the debate, therefore, would be a theology rooted in the Church and the regard which God holds for all people.

The second theological approach is connected with the first, in that it recognizes the 'rights' of young people, but it is rooted in the tradition of liberation. The liberation of young people is related to institutional power, but also to the raising of social consciousness and theological creativity amongst young people themselves. Young people are marginalized just like many other groups. A theology from their lived experience can be a source of hope and social transformations. A Theology of Youth thus has its place alongside Black Theology, Asian Theology and Feminist Theology. Again this approach is advocated by Kujawa; it is also to be seen in the work of the Roman Catholic, Michael Warren.

Whilst I am not ruling these two lines of theological argument out of play in discourses concerning young people, I am not convinced that they offer a politically viable route for negotiating the place of youth in the Church. To speak frankly, I am increasingly of the mind that the Church will only listen to young people when it is forced to realize that its own survival demands it. It is really only self-interest that will persuade those with 'say so' to advocate listening to young people. In many churches in the UK young people between the ages of 16 and 25 are generally regarded as being extinct. Like dinosaurs, there may well have been a day when large herds travelled across the plains of the Church Hall and gathered to feed at the Altar, but now those days are long gone. As the Archbishop of Canterbury says on regular occasions, 'The Church is only one generation away from extinction.'

All of this concentrates the mind wonderfully. It doesn't take a theological or sociological wizard to work out that for significant sections of the Church of England the writing is on the wall. Thus, at this present time, young people are starting to find their way onto the agendas of synods, bishops' standing committees and Archbishop's Initiatives. Interestingly, young people are far from being extinct from evangelical and charismatic Anglican churches. At festivals such as the Anglican Soul Survivor, and at summer youth camps organized by groups such as the Church Youth Fellowships Association, young people between the ages of 14 and 25 gather in their thousands. Faced with these kinds of success catholics and liberals are slowly starting to turn their attention to young people. A little while back I was invited to address a group of ordinands at a theological college. The college is generally recognized as representing the more liberal/catholic tradition in the Church. The training session took place a week before the group were due to leave to join their parishes. I started the seminar with the expectation that, given the theological interests of the group, I would be involved in a discussion dealing with topics such as young people in society, the social and political stresses on youth and the role of the Church in challenging unjust structures. Not a bit of it. The chief concern was 'How do we get the young people into Church?' One student asked me right out, 'What is the secret of the evangelicals?'

As far as I can tell, the situation in the Church of England is repeated in many parts of the Anglican Communion. In many countries those who occupy a broadly Anglican position find themselves under threat from successful and lively non-Anglican charismatic groups. Despite the best efforts of bishops and clergy, the Pied Piper is leading our children away. At the same time a number of evangelical Anglicans have themselves adopted the spirituality and worship styles associated with the many 'waves of charismatic renewal'. It does not surprise me that it is these churches which often attract large numbers of young people. The dilemma I have heard expressed goes something like, 'Do we have to adopt guitars, singing in tongues, and that charismatic stuff to attract young people? Because if that is the case I don't want to do it.'

At this point I should probably declare where I stand on some of these issues. I understand that for many Anglicans the liturgy and tradition of the Church is extremely important and meaningful. To a large extent I share that view. At the same time I, like many young people, have found a renewal of spiritual experience through involvement in charismatic worship. I experience very little tension between these two aspects of my spiritual life. I recognize, however, that for those unconvinced of the charismatic cause the problem is yet to be solved. In such circumstances it is a seemingly tough choice: how do we keep our young people and yet remain Anglican in tradition? I am not about to offer any direct solution, but it seems sensible to at least attempt to consult those young people who are currently within the Anglican Church to see what they have to say. Again, such a move often comes out of desperation. On the whole the Church seeks the advice of young people when all other options have run out.

Desperate the Church may be, but still, it will only listen if it feels that young people have something valuable and helpful to say. The problem is that not every young person is articulate, together, creative, energetic or, indeed, terribly spiritual. There is a difference between listening to someone because it is a pastoral responsibility and listening to someone because you think they might have the answer to a problem. It is this confusion between pastoral mode and political mode which goes to the heart of the issue. Pastoral mode is a basic expression of love and concern; political mode is about effecting change. When the Diocesan Bishop arrives at the youth camp he is almost certainly in pastoral mode, when the congregation attend the monthly youth service they are expressing pastoral concern, and when the local vicar attends the youth barbecue he or she is doing the same. All of these activities are fundamental to the life of the Church and they are part of expressing the body of Christ. But they are pastoral not political.

The dire straits of much of Church work amongst young people in the UK (and, indeed, in many other parts of the world) changes all of that. Frankly, bishops want solutions. Clergy want to see the return of young people to the pews. Parents want to see their children eager to attend Church. The questions which arise from these facts are essentially political. 'What must be done to effect change?' This is the starting point for a real dialogue between young people and those who hold power within the structures of the Church.

A starting point it may be, but the end point it is not. Pastoral mode predicates listening as an end in itself. Listening is self-evidently good. The purpose of such pastoral encounters is 'being heard'. The political mode is about effecting change. When operating in political mode bishops, clergy and even Archbishops want solutions. They are not just passing the time of day, they are genuinely looking for answers – after all, the future of the parish, the diocese, the Church itself is perhaps at stake.

Now the dynamic has changed. Young people are at the table and asked to contribute. The matters in hand may be various: why do young people not attend evensong? What would attract young people from the local school on the parish pilgrimage? How can we get young people involved in our campaign to change the conditions of refuges? What would the Mothers Union have to do to attract more teenage mothers?

Maybe this is a Church of my dreams. But there are a number of indications that my hopeful imaginings are not entirely off mark. There are a significant number of key decision makers who are starting to recognize that work amongst children and young people is a major priority for the Anglican Church. This really puts the ball in the court of young people around the Communion. What have they got to say? Are young people capable of offering direction, energy and life to the Anglican Church? If many in the ministry and in authority are at a loss as to the way forward, what can young people offer?

This chapter is written out of the conviction that the answer to these questions is 'yes'. Yes, young people really do have something to contribute to the life of the Church. In fact my exposure to young people from around the Communion has convinced me that those currently active within the Anglican Church have a good deal to bring to the table. This chapter is based upon a series of conversations with young Anglicans. These young people were gathered together in 1997 in London and in Lampeter to discuss the issues related to the forthcoming Lambeth Conference. As part of my own preparation for the Conference I spent time talking with some of these young people. The interviews were conducted over a relatively short period on a one-to-one basis. The views the young people expressed are not to be taken as official communications, they are simply individual expressions of faith and conviction. That said, the young people were aware that their views were, in some way, to be conveyed to the bishops who were due to gather in 1998.

## The Voices of Young People

It is worth saying that these young people and young adults were a fairly rarefied grouping. Any young person financed by their Province to travel to such a gathering is by definition, connected to the Anglican structures. But, even so, I was struck by the Anglican orthodoxy of those I met. Whilst they were from radically different countries, cultures and traditions within Anglicanism the young people seemed united on three key areas: the Gospel, justice, and the Church. This chapter is organized around these three areas. In each of the sections following I will quote the young people at length as well as discuss the implications of what they have to say.

GOSPEL

A number of the young people showed a considerable commitment to themselves as 'gospel people'. This was expressed as a desire to be active in the ministry of the Church.

The message that I may want the Lambeth bishops to consider is to accept the voice of even the smallest in the church of God, so that the youth are not taken as people who will do things for the kingdom of God tomorrow, but are taken as people who will do what pertains to the kingdom of God today and even tomorrow so that the kingdom may look balanced.

Jesse Matuyiwanaky, Kenya

Jesse and others saw themselves as part of the coming of God's Kingdom. They are willing to be active in serving the Kingdom in their countries. They are anxious to play their part. For some this meant being active in preaching the Gospel. James Moses Lado from Sudan saw young people as an active part of the church's ministry in his country.

... especially in my country, the young people are the most people to go outside to preach the gospel, and that is why we really need that our bishops to look to the young people because they are the young generation to go out and preach the gospel ...

The energy, commitment and enthusiasm of young people represent a major source of hope for the Church. There is a clear conviction amongst many of these young people that they are willing to give a significant part of their lives to the Christian faith. At the same time they seem to feel that they need the wider Church and, in particular, bishops to give them permission. They are waiting to be asked to get involved. As they looked forward to the Lambeth Conference they hoped for an invitation from the bishops to get even more involved in mission. Eric Bawingen from the Philippines expresses the sentiments of many in the group when he says:

I would say that the bishops should give more prioritization to the courses or to the works of the young people. The young people have potential, they are more an asset than liability. So I would say that they should hear the voices of these young people.

Ready for action they might be, but many of those I interviewed saw the size of the challenge before the Church. There is a realization that social and political realities are complex and on the whole the Church struggles to connect with the lives of young people. Yazeed Said from Palestine reflects on the mission of the Church in his context.

> Well I think it's very difficult really to do work successfully in the context of the land in which we live, because we do have projects, we do have a youth officer, we do have a youth director, what we call a youth director in the diocese and I believe he is doing some work. He is gathering people, he is gathering young children, but it isn't easy to go and tell them we need you in the church. It's very difficult because they don't see in the church, they don't meet their needs, they don't meet what they want, they meet something, as others have said already, very old fashioned, very traditional, something that doesn't belong to the world, doesn't belong to their culture, so the church, I believe, has to go where the people are. If they are in pubs, the church has to go to pubs, if they are at schools the church has to exist in the school, if they are playing outside, if they are in the streets, wherever they are the church has to go and follow them. The church should not expect those young people to come and say, I need the church, because the church have other needs, the church have to meet other things as well, sorry, the young people have to meet other things in the world.

The challenge is pretty clear. Young people are living their lives in places outside of the normal activities of the Church. If we are to be gospel people amongst these young people then we need to find ways to live out the message of Christ in the places where they are. This involves a radical change in the priorities of Church life. We need to go out to young people. No longer can the Church expect young people to turn up at our services. But going to where young people are is really only the first part of the challenge. Meeting young people in their lived experience necessarily involves connecting with the issues and concerns which characterize their lives. Brian Williams from Argentina is clear that this demands that the Church starts to interact with some of the more difficult social and moral questions of our societies.

> I think the church is not helping with things like drugs, drinks, sex. The young people need [a] guide in those things.

11

> The parents are not any more the reference, and they need some reference and the church should be that reference, but actually it is not.

If the Gospel is to become a life-changing reality in the lives of young people then it will have to be heard and experienced as 'Good News' by young people in their lived experience. According to Brian Williams young people need a point of reference. If the Church is to fulfil this function then it can only do so by encouraging individuals to commit themselves to living out the Kingdom in the social world of young people. This, of course, means being in touch with young people outside of the Church, but it also means that those involved in such ministry must be equipped to connect their faith to contemporary culture. It has long been my own concern that theological education needs to take the lived experience of young people much more seriously. Somehow we need to develop the theological resources to train our priests and lay people to respond to the rhythm of young people's lives. This does not represent a 'dumbing down' of theological education. On the contrary, it is a commitment to rigorous theological reflection upon some of the more pressing and complex questions of the age.

JUSTICE

There is a strong commitment on the part of these young people to see the Gospel expressed in terms of justice and transformation. Louis Amible Muvunyi is charged with development of youth work in Rwanda. He is critical of the history of the Church in his country and yet, faced with a country torn apart by civil war and with the after effects of genocide, Louis is convinced that young people under the power of Christ are a source of hope.

> People are wondering how can a country like Rwanda which has been known as a Christian country, how can people kill one another to that extent? But what I can say is that most Christians were just nominal Christians and we are now preaching a message which I can say, it's a message which is telling Christians to change. To be a Christian is to change, not just come to church and to sit and to sing and to hear sermons, but to be a Christian is to change, and that is the

message which I am communicating in my country and in young people's work.

I believe young people, I think young people, it's a potential force I believe, which can transform my country, but we have programmes because most of the young people are ignorant, they are uneducated. You find that they have no proper education background, they have no skills, their mothers are unemployed so you find that most of the young people need to be educated so that they can really be agents of peace, agents of reconciliation, agents of development in my country.

Kagiso Molefe reflected very similar hopes when I asked him about the role of young people in the changes which had recently taken place in his country of South Africa.

Yes, in some ways they did, perhaps by, sort of, encouraging other young people not to surrender or to give up when the situation was really bad. But perhaps, again, I need to say that we did have problems in terms of reaching out to the white young people and perhaps it is because of the situation then, but it was not possible for both black and white to meet together, but we did try our utmost best as the black young people, to reach out as we are at the particular moment, trying to reach out and perhaps reconciling both races to come together, and together I think as the young people in the church of the province of Southern Africa, we have the ability to help reshape our country, who are still in the process of changing, who are still in the process of reconciliation, and I think the church is looking upon us as young people to bring that sense of reconciliation among the nation.

There are huge challenges in countries such as Rwanda or South Africa, but young Anglicans share a common concern to get involved and to change the social situations in whatever country in which they find themselves. Joanne Foster from Scotland speaks in very similar terms about Glasgow.

I think that, well certainly there are programmes, to begin with, particularly in some of the poorer areas of the diocese which is Glasgow and Galloway, where I come from. There are people working with some of the poorest people in Scotland and they are working with the young people, with young mothers, with drug addicts, and with all the people really on the fringes of our society. I think the church needs to work on this. There is almost an insularity, I find, about Scottish Anglicanism, Scottish Episcopalianism, and perhaps we're not as confident about reaching out to people as we should be. Richard Holloway, [Bishop of Edinburgh], described our church as the church for sinners and everybody who thinks they're sorted out can go and be members of other churches. And I think perhaps we need to put that across more, that you don't have to have your life organised to be part of the church. In fact, you know, if your life's not organised maybe the church is where you need to be.

The desire to see change come about in their own situation is very evident. The hope that the Gospel can connect with people who realize that their lives are not sorted out is felt deeply. At the same time there is a realization that the Gospel demands that the Church is active in the wider political and economic sphere. Joanne again.

I think the first thing is, deal with world debt. I don't think in the north and the west of Christianity, I'm not sure how we can hold our heads up as part of the Anglican communion when effectively we condone the loan-shark behaviour of the world banks. We wouldn't allow it in our own communities. The churches wouldn't allow somebody to lend somebody a hundred pounds and charge two hundred pounds in interest, but we let it happen abroad. We will let children be uneducated, we will let children die for lack of medication, rather than stand up and say what you're doing is wrong. And I think we need to support, certainly I know Christian Aid is working towards this, working towards getting supermarkets to use fairly traded products and calling a Jubilee for debt, and I think that's where it has to start. We're not all equal and we never will be, but I think we have to make the playing fields as level as we possibly can.

The young people were looking to the Bishops gathering at Lambeth to make a stand on the issue of debt. In addition, there were a number of issues of justice and human rights which were close to the heart of the group. Rui Pedro Luz Soares from Portugal was particularly concerned with human rights in East Timor.

> One of the most important issues that we'd like the Bishops to talk about was the East Timor issue, because we feel that the European countries they are not supporting that cause, and every day East Timor people are being killed by the hands of the military, Indonesian military, and it [is] an issue that concerns us a lot. . . . This place East Timor is being a very forgotten place by the West world and many countries continue supporting the Indonesian army, like the United States, like England of course, and many countries and we would like very much for the Bishops to make a statement and try to stop this killing and at least pray for the East Timor people.

CHURCH

Gospel people committed to preaching and the expression of the Good News in works of justice and social action these young people may be, but they are also young people with a strong sense of affiliation to the Anglican Church. Their experience of the Church, however, was mixed. For some, involvement in the Church was a very positive aspect of their lives.

> There's quite a lot of young people, because Brazil is a country of young people so that's why we have so many young people in the church. The whole liturgy is very opened and very flexible, so we can always participate very well during the service and we used to help in the other social projects that the church is offering to the other people.
>
> Martha Tessman, Brazil

Martha's experience of the Church is not felt by all of the young people. Sourbabh Pholia from Bangladesh appreciates the connections the Church offers between young and old, but there are stresses and strains.

> Sometimes what I have seen in some parishes, they don't have a good relationship with the old people and, between the old

people and the young people, because, I think it's for understanding. Because what is their idea of the old people ideas,
that is agreeing to their thinking, but nowadays what the
young people are thinking, they want to be more open and
they want some changes in their church, so it brings sometimes clashes and sometimes misunderstandings there also
between the young and the old people in our churches. Not
all the churches, but in some churches.

Sarah Arndt from Wales recognizes that these problems sometimes
result in young people moving outside of the worshipping life of
the Church.

... the young people go through a stage where, they go
through that age where they question who they are, what
they believe, what the world's about and they just need time
to reflect and look at the whole picture and the church
doesn't really fit it in, or it doesn't relate to what they're going
through, and it's something perhaps the church needs to
look at.

Relating to the stages of adolescence can be as stressful for the
Church as it is for some parents. These kinds of tensions, it should
be recognized, will be structured differently in other cultures and
contexts. Social and economic changes impact variously upon
families and communities. An example of this is the way that in
some African countries traditional family structures are under
stress from the impact of urbanization, while in the UK the steady
rise in the number of divorces means that many young people grow
up in extended family networks with step-parents, half-brothers
and half-sisters, etc. Life experiences are varied, but generational
tension and perhaps conflict remains a prevailing theme. Alongside
generational problems there is a globalized youth-oriented media.
Satelite TV, film, radio and the internet deliver products for
consumption to a youth market. Nike, Coca-Cola, McDonald's,
Levi's are consumed as objects of desire and pleasure by young
people around the world. Youth subcultures are constructed by
such consumption.

Many of the young people expressed the desire for the Church to
be more 'open'. This is not just an openness to young people as the
younger generation, for a good few it represents a desire for the

worship of the Church to reflect their particular cultural tastes. The construction identity through youth subcultures therefore begins to impact upon Christian spirituality. Central to this is the kind of music used in Church. Richard Tucker from Jamaica reflects upon young people in his Church.

> ... there are many, they come to the church for various reasons, because they were really brought up in the church, their families have been going to the church for many years, so they automatically go to church, and for those who go to church because they really want to. They feel that they gain something from the church, but within that number there are those who are becoming disillusioned because the church, to them, it is too traditional, it is old fashioned, and there need to be changes and they have been stifled in terms of their ideas, in implementing new ideas, and so, some leave because they feel that the church is not as lively as they would want to see it.

Richard sees the way forward in his country in the development of worship which makes use of the music which is popular amongst many of the young people.

> Slowly we are trying to do things with our liturgy, with our worship, to make it more indigenous to what is happening in Jamaica, and one of the ways of doing that is through music, but when persons hear of reggae music, they think, reggae music and the church don't mix, they have a particular view of reggae music and it is not within the church, but what can be done and what is being done in some areas, instruments, indigenous instruments, drums are being used. Steel pans are also being used within the worship context and persons now realise that this is not something which is totally bad, you know, but it is something that can enhance the worship event and the worship experience.

For some in the Church the use of reggae music is seen as sinful and of the world.

> That is the impression that many persons get when they hear of reggae music and hence that is not something for the

church, but what can be done, reggae music is Jamaican and we have to do things in order to make our worship and our liturgy Jamaican and the music is one such way, and it has been done in such a way that Christian words can be put to certain reggae beats and it comes across in a very meaningful way, you know, to many persons who experience this.

... there actually is a setting, a reggae mass, you know, so that is already there, but not many churches use this mass setting because of the stigma which is attached to reggae music. There are some priests who, should I say, are forward thinking, who will utilise this particular mass setting and from our reports it came across very well, not just with the young people but with other members of the congregation.

The use of reggae in Jamaica is not just a youth 'thing'; it is a matter of contextualization. Youth culture impacts upon the wider community. The discourse of the media, and the subcultural groups which generate and consume the cultural products of the media, is generated out of a rapidly changing 'youth scene'. The effect of this is that 'youth culture' is transformed into a more widely consumed 'popular culture'. By adopting reggae music as a setting for the mass, young people are leading the way in the development of an indigenous Anglicanism. Increasingly it is the case that youth culture is the embryonic popular culture of the wider community. To connect with young people is to engage missiologically with whole communities. This is not simply a matter of style, it is a deeper theological statement about the Church truly being expressed in culture. Catherine Morrison from Canada makes this very clear in her reflections upon the role that indigenous peoples can play in the life of the Church in Canada.

The thing that is different when indigenous peoples have ownership in the church is that is when the church is most fully realised. The church is just a club when people go there every Sunday and don't take part. They just sing the hymns and listen to the sermon and do nothing in themselves or of themselves for the church. Indigenous peoples have a gift to offer mainstream Canadian Anglicans and also the Anglican communion.

The issues at stake in connecting with popular cultures, be that of indigenous peoples or of contemporary youth culture, are essentially the same. How do we connect with the cultural activity of the community and yet remain faithful to Christ? How can we embrace the cultural expressions of popular culture and yet remain 'Anglican'? These questions are basic to Church history and mission studies. What is rarely mentioned in theological studies is that the cultural context of young people offers an interpretative key to these and related issues. It is my belief that young people are, in many ways, in the vanguard of the sensibilities which can lead the Church upon this journey. To the extent that the Anglican Church wishes to be contextualized in culture, it will have to take young people seriously as their guides and creative energy in this enterprise. In many cases this life and energy start outside of the Church. Andrew from Watford in England sees a good many things which are exciting but, on the whole, they are happening in the parachurch agencies and charismatic groups.

> . . . in terms of youth worship, youth ministry, youth work a lot is going on outside churches in terms of preaching, ministry, worship. And I think all that needs to be done now is to bring the youth into the churches. There have been many events such as 'The Champion of the World' event at Wembley stadium which drew thousands of people. The entire Wembley stadium was filled and for eight hours or so there was a time of worship led by the worship band singing, four different bands, four worship leaders, plus a speaker and the stadium was filled with youth. Now all I think needs to be done now is to get other less known bands, bands who aren't recording, but just being able to play the music that the youth appreciate, but in churches. To bring back worship into churches because there is so much going on now with celebrations in big community centres, it just needs to be moved out of there and back into the places of worship that have been established for so many . . . hundreds of years.

Andrew sees that the Church is held back by its structures and its leadership. If change is to come then these people need to get behind young people.

I'd like to see less emphasis on the hierarchy of clergy. I think everyone regardless of age, and their position in church, needs to have their voice, needs to say something, what they feel, share their experiences, their views with others so churches, I mean mine isn't one, but churches where the minister just does everything, and there may be a couple of people who read lessons . . .

I'd like to say that the hierarchy within the clergy system needs to be lessened so that people in the church, the parishioners themselves, the lay people, the worshippers get a voice and particularly in the youth worship scene, because there are so many people, it seems to me, that want to worship in church but they can't find a church that is suited to them, and so they have this problem with the fact that Anglican churches are sort of old and established and have hymns which don't appeal to them, but if the minister going out to people is, if his work is lessened and more work placed on just general parishioners, particularly young people, they can go out to young people and say, 'Look we're not old fuddy duddy's, we haven't been around for ages, we don't have grey hair, please come and worship, we're not an old church we're a new church, we're today's church', then I think the church will have a future.

Young Anglicans feel that they are in an old Church and they want things to change. Vandra Harris from Australia is clear that those in authority need to take the risk and bring about change.

. . . I would like to say that young people should be heard and not laid back especially in the church, if there has to be change in the church for young people to go forward, there can't be a change if a change isn't allowed.

## On Message

It was sobering to speak with these young people. Their commitment to the Christian faith was inspiring. Here were young Anglicans from around the world and yet they had a remarkable unity of vision. These were people committed to seeing the Gospel proclaimed in both word and deed. They were also deeply committed to the Church, and to the Anglican Church in particular, if, at times, they were critical of the way things are. Yet at the same time their concerns seemed to be distinctively Anglican. It is interesting to compare their comments with those of official Anglican positions. The Anglican Consultative Council (ACC) report *Mission in a Broken World* sets out a vision for mission in the following terms.

> There has been a consistent view of mission repeated by ACC, the Lambeth Conference, the Primates' meeting and others in recent years, which defines mission in a four-fold way:
> The mission of the Church is:
> a) to proclaim the good news of the Kingdom;
> b) to teach, baptise and nurture new believers;
> c) to respond to human need by loving service;
> d) to seek to transform the unjust structures of society.
>
> (ACC 1990, p.101)

It is remarkable how much in accord with these statements the young people appear to be. Their concerns and those of the rest of the Anglican Communion are very closely linked. Young Anglicans, it would seem, to use a contemporary political term, are 'on message'. My own feeling after talking with these young people was an overwhelming sense of connection with the Anglican Communion. I was filled with a sense of joy about my own Anglican identity. These young people were certainly worth listening to. They had something to say. If the future of the Church and the proclamation of the Gospel is really to be placed in the hands of young people such as these, the future looks bright indeed.

# 2

# Incarnational Youth Ministry
## in terms of Identity, Culture and Stories

### *Dean Borgman*

'Youth are not tomorrow's leaders; they should be leaders of the Church today!' This slogan has been echoed around the world until it is in danger of becoming a useless cliché. We must, therefore, 'unpack' the phrase and examine its meaning. Is it realistic to see young people as Church leaders? Do they want to be Church leaders? Do they have the time and expertise to do so?

First of all, let's listen to young people themselves. Realize that young people, as any group or subculture, do not speak with a common voice, but prize their individuality and their particular types of youthful culture. Around the world there are school-leavers, homeless youth, wealthy teenagers sent away to boarding schools, athletes, young people working hard to pass their exams while engaged in part-time jobs or family responsibilities, academic honours students, computer whizzes, and skateboarders hanging out downtown. Worldwide, only a few of them are at Church. We must listen to them all.

Here is what the young people of the Diocese of Massachusetts in the US decided they wanted to say to adult Church leaders in 1990.

> We are young people in the ambiguous place between child-hood and adulthood, we need to be recognized as such. Though we face the devastating issues inherent in today's society, we don't have the experience to deal with them without people more mature than we are ... YOUTH – we are told we are difficult to deal with. Although we are regarded

as 'just children' we are facing very adult issues. We often must make very mature decisions about: Drugs, Sexuality, Prejudice, Child Abuse, Parental Battering, Peer Pressure, Faith. These are certainly not childlike issue and we face them on a daily basis. We need all the understanding and help that you can give us. . . . We want support. We want your trust, your respect – your love. We want to develop coping mechanisms, and decision-making skills. . . . We believe that through faith, understanding, communication with and support from OUR church, we all can fulfill our mission to love and serve the Lord.[1]

The 13 young people heard here are a select group who, not only attend Church, but made further commitments to serve. *Listen* to what they are saying. They are not asking to take part in long committee meetings or to be treated exactly like adults. Their sense of their identity is as YOUTH (which they have capitalized). The stress they feel stems from their difficult position in a complex world. Their problems are symptoms of that stress. And what they want most from adults and the Church are understanding and respect, trust and love. All my experience with young people confirms this fact: they neither want to be treated like children or adults, but as people in a complex and exciting transitional period – with a culture all its own. 'Our world is different from the world of our parents,' they tell me. And in that world they are, first of all, working out their own personal identities within friendship groups.

---

To serve youth, the Church must first listen, not only to its own young people, but to those of the entire youth culture. Listening takes time, and it must seek real understanding and exhibit genuine respect.

---

*Identity*

From Kenya, Adam Chepkwony sees the first issue of youth as the identity crisis:

The search for personal identity is crucial in the life of every young person. The identity crisis can be said to be the cause of practically all the problems affecting the youth. Their rebellion and disobedience against authority, and in particular to their parents, is not so much to defy them but a search for their own identity and autonomy. To understand the agonies that young people go through during this difficult period of their lives, we need to let them speak for themselves.[2]

Chepkwony supplies statements from male and female teenagers – about their frustrations with parents, others and self, regarding sexual energies, restrictions and moods – which, he says, 'epitomize the struggles African youth undergo in their unceasing search for identity.'[3] It is clear that young people live in their own world with their own kind of relationships. In that context they are working out their sexual, vocational and spiritual identities.[4]

In striking contrast to animals, human beings are completely dependent while becoming independent human beings. Animals are born with a large supply of instinctive behaviours; a baby has a remarkably small number of instinctive behaviours. Human socialization is a complicated affair. While animals instinctively 'act their species'; our infants have to *learn* how to be human. Adulthood demands thousands of learned behaviours.

As children pass puberty, they have a new (and sometimes exaggerated) sense of self-hood. At this place in human development, they have an increased need to differentiate themselves from others and to integrate their own sense of self (self-image, value system, schedule and responsibilities, sense of personal strengths and potential).[5]

Traditional societies provide complementary social systems for their children. Extended family, village or town, traditional work and school patterns, rites of passage, cultural stories – all these give youth a consistent value system and expected roles or social status. Security, time and, perhaps most important, designated mentors help a young person become an adult.

War or urbanization can tear away these supportive social systems. Both war and urbanization weaken or destroy extended families, rites of passage, caring mentors and meaningful apprenticeships. Western media add another disruption and further confusion of values. Without communal security and caring mentors, young people are rushed to pseudo-maturity. Forced to learn by imitation rather than integration, they develop an internal mosaic of values. Both their personal identities and their personal boundaries are weak. David Elkind describes the difficulties and unique stress among contemporary, postmodern youth.

> In some situations where we do not know the rules, it is generally considered wise to follow the example of others who are familiar with the situation. (Consider the anomie of warfare, urban streets, suburban parties and the media scene.) But this type of learning is not adaptive when it comes to constructing a sense of personal identity. A sense of self – constructed by the simple compilation of feelings, thoughts, and beliefs appropriated from others amounts to a *patchwork* self. A young person who has constructed a sense of self in this way has no inner sense of self to fall back on for guidance and direction. Such individuals are easily influenced by others, both because they have no internal gyroscope and because they have developed the habit of following others rather than making their own decisions. Each new situation is a fresh challenge, and they are always looking for external direction – which may not be forthcoming. Adolescents with a patchwork self are vulnerable to stress because . . . they lack the history of differentiation and higher-order integration that would prepare them to deal with new situations on the basis of past experiences and reality constructions.[6]

The single largest problem contemporary young people face is stress. Smoking, alcohol and drug abuse are primarily attempts to relieve pervasive pressures – young people say. Unfortunately, many negative behaviours, intended to relieve stress, only produce more stress.

The future is an uncertain one for many youth today. Vocational identity is built upon a clear sense of personal strengths, interests and values. Young people are forced to put together values from fragmented parts of their social life: their family compartment, school compartment, religious compartment, athletic or work compartment and social compartments. These values may be in striking contradiction; yet 'true' for them in their varied experiences.

A group of athletes we interviewed were attending a religious convention. They responded positively to values regarding Church involvement, critiquing negative messages in the media, and sexual integrity. Personal conversations with them revealed, however, that they expected to be back in the city contradicting many of these values that very weekend. Yet, while admitting differences in behaviour, they saw no problem, or even tension, in the contradiction. Many young people expect 'church truth' to be different from 'school truth' and different still from 'social truth' among their friends. Experts have described this increasing compartmentalization of values in terms such as 'pseudo-maturity', 'multiple-personae', 'patchwork selves', and 'particle persons'.

In most urban societies, the extended family has been replaced with a nuclear family, with both parents working. For many young people now, there is no extended family and village to help. What takes their place? Greater responsibility has been placed on schools. But, increasingly, postmodern youth find in their friends and the media substitutes for family and education.

It is important to consider the social systems now supporting our children's growth. How does each of the following social systems influence the quest for identity of young people in your social context?[7]

- Family
- Community
- Schools (and day-care)
- Media
- Church (maybe)
- Friends

Athletics, music or drama, employment and youth organizations may also enter the picture. For too many youth, the streets and drugs, crime and the criminal justice system are central. It is very important for the Church and youth ministry to consider this picture carefully. It clarifies youth ministry as a composite of missionary work, social work and pastoral nurture.

Children *play* at adult life. Their toys and dolls represent things they see adults doing and provide opportunities to pretend they have the necessary skills for the adult world. Jesus commented on children playing 'weddings and funerals' in the market place.[8]

Adolescents or youth *practice* adult life. Day-care is a play centre; a teenage hangout a practice center. In school, through part-time jobs, parties and dating, teenagers and young adults are trying out what someday will be more permanent careers and relationships. It is also the scene in which they develop a clearer sense of personal identity.

---

The Church is not a major social system for young people growing up today. Most youth are not institutionally inclined and are quite critical of an institution that would divide them denominationally and impose expectations from a context other than their immediate subculture. But they *are* spiritually and relationally inclined. Young people respond to adults who care to enter their world and relate to them. Their spiritual identities can be clarified and influenced by adults who care enough to enter their world and take the time for relationships.

---

## Culture

When war forces children to become instant adults, it is a social crime. This has happened all over the world. It is estimated that 85,000 children and teenagers are heads of families in Rwanda alone. When governments and relief agencies cannot deal adequately with such need, the Church must be especially attentive.

When radical changes in families and media rob children of their innocence and any real childhood, rushing them into pseudo-adulthood without time, security or mentors to allow for healthy development, it is also a social failure. The Church cannot simply say, 'It shouldn't be like that', or 'We have some healthy families and children so it is no immediate concern of ours.' The fact is our children and youth are more influenced by negative social forces than we care to admit. We must become more sensitive to children, and culturally aware.

Culture is all learned behaviour passed on over generations through the social systems we have mentioned. Like individuals, cultures need to survive, flourish and reproduce. Cultures are based on common needs and common situations. We speak of a culture as the way any people collectively meet their needs in a particular context with some common belief system.[9]

When any group in a society feels their needs unattended to, they may create, consciously or unconsciously, a subculture that meets their needs, a style of life that speaks to them and for them. Caught between childhood and adulthood by developmental and social factors, youth seek music, entertainment, fashions, language, humour and more to be their own. In a sense, it is their voice, and the more they are marginalized and not listened to, the louder the volume of that cultural voice may become. It is their world, their values, their frustration and pain, their hopes and dreams that are being lamented and celebrated in their music and lifestyle. It is *their* youth culture.

The youth culture (including the many youth subcultures within it) is more segregated from adult society, more influenced by media and more globalized that ever before. No philosophy of Christian Education or Youth Ministry will change that fact. Certainly we can create small counter-cultures in our parishes, and these may exhibit, at least in the short term, very positive results. But it is not the answer for reaching all youth everywhere. Nor does it fully prepare our young people to live in the world without being part of the negative aspects of postmodern society.

---

Young people are dying, in some cases literally, for want of dialogue. Their cultural and personal stories are of crucial importance. But personal stories must intersect with the stories of others and, at some point, with the Great Story: the Good News of God's love. Put quite simply and starkly, the Church is too busy and fearful to enter the culture of our young people. So we only work with those who come to us.

---

## Incarnational Youth Ministry

A busy young journalist had just moved into a new apartment in the heat of summer. As he was finishing up, he met a new neighbour and was invited to a barbecue just a few houses away. After meeting the hosts of the party, he sat alone relieving his thirst and hunger. Suddenly he was aware of a small girl in a bathing suit next to him with her arms upraised, as if seeking attention or a hug. New to the neighbourhood and covered with barbecue sauce, he turned away until she left and similarly raised her hands to someone else, who also ignored her.

Completing his refreshing lunch, the writer heard a terrible scream and saw people rushing in the direction of a garden swimming pool. Soon there was also the siren of an emergency medical vehicle. All efforts were too late to revive the little girl in a bathing suit. The writer later learned that she had been caught in the centre of a particularly bitter divorce. Upon further enquiries he found out that the child had once before fallen into the pool, been pulled out, and made the centre of attention for an afternoon. The journalist wrote this true story as a human interest piece, and perhaps as a bit of personal confession. For the Church it has far greater significance.

I remember having a particularly difficult time getting close to my youngest of four children. Maybe we are too alike and strong in personality. Anyway, she resented my discipline and tended to withdraw to her friends. She was about nine or ten when I was one day attempting to deepen our relationship. No matter how I tried, I received little response from her. I had gone into her bedroom, sat on her bed, but still we weren't talking. I remember my pain and frustration and her blank look.

My ministry was teaching about relating to young people, and I couldn't even get through to my own daughter. In despair, I almost cried out, 'Christen, you and your friends, Ali and Cindy, stay in this room for hours talking, and you can't even talk to me for ten minutes?' But no response was forthcoming. 'What is it you talk about in here?' 'Oh,' she replied, 'we talk about Kenny and Barbie.' Somehow it dawned on my old mind that I too might get on the floor with my daughter and see what her dolls were all about. For the next hour, it seemed, I listened and learned how Christen and her friends would play out individuals and couples of their fifth-grade life. I was now in her world, down on her level, listening to the inside story. I was even given insights into a child's view of romance and sexuality!

These two stories have a great deal to do with youth ministry and the Gospel according to John. For 'the Word was made flesh and lived among us'.[10] The great Word, which was with God and was God, came into our world, noticed us, sat down with us, and began sharing stories. That's what the wedding party is about in John 2, and what was going on between Jesus and the Samaritan woman in the fourth chapter of John. And it is the same Word who says, 'As the Father has sent me, so I send you.'[11] This is incarnational youth ministry, and provides principles for recruiting youth leaders and carrying on the mission of the Church within the subcultures of youth.

The Church is always threatened by the occupational hazards to which the scribes and Pharisees succumbed. They expected people to come to them, to enter their subculture, to hear a religious voice from outside their common culture. But Jesus turned that method of ministry on its head! He went to people first, learned their language and concerns, and taught them on their own terms, in their own cultural language. And as Christ planted the seeds of the Gospel, he expected the Church to take root in new ways in each human culture. Old wine skins were not able to hold the liberating, healing and empowering Word and Spirit.

Few religious leaders have been as popular as Jesus Christ was, at least for a while. He attracted both friends and enemies. Yet, in the midst of those crowds, Jesus always noticed individuals and took time with them. We read something like this again and again: now a certain woman, a blind man, a leper, a widow, a child. Troubled teenagers today need the same kind of personal and time-consuming attention. With Christ, we must put people before programmes.

Incarnational ministry is a ministry of presence. It leaves a world of privilege and security (as Christ left heaven's glory for service that would end in humiliation, rejection and death)[12] to enter an unknown culture of others. Incarnational ministry interprets love as a four-lettered word spelt T-I-M-E. It pays attention to rich and poor, leaders and followers, high-achievers and youth-at-risk, and expects its ministry to be relevant to all in between.

Incarnational ministry is relational. It realizes that teenage years put more emphasis on relationships than any other age. It sees peer relationships as crucial for the clarification of personal identity, and adult mentors crucial to positive growth.

Incarnational ministry is in the style of Jesus and successful mission efforts ever since. It matches the mandates of Scripture with the crying needs of the world. Young people and adult leaders working together today will create relevant youth ministry. Caring mentors will provide young people with a safe place, where a young person can hear a friend telling her story and being affirmed for it, until she has the courage to tell her own story and, in that context, hear the story of God's love. All experts today see the need for nurturing mentors giving young people time and space to work out their identities and callings in life. The first expert to advise this style of ministry, by word and example, was Jesus.

---

Look at street children in Lagos, Johannesburg or Calcutta; observe skateboarders in London or New York; watch surfers in South Africa, California or Australia; listen to the rap of homeboys in ghettos or townships; mix with dancing youth in South America; meet third culture children at expensive international schools. You know they can only be reached when someone goes to them. This is the challenge of youth ministry today; this is the Church's mission.

---

*Obstacles to Incarnational Ministry*

One of the saddest lines in the Bible (though this is not to exegete the passage) is the Lord's lament, 'And I sought for anyone . . . who would stand in the breach . . . but I found no one'.[13] There is worldwide acknowledgement of a youth crisis. In new ways, even secular societies are willing to receive aid from the Church and Christians willing to serve the common good. Why, then, do we falter?

One reason is fear. We hear adults say, 'Look at their hostility; listen to the words of their vicious rap (or rock) music. There's no way I would go near them!' Many pastors in developing nations see young people with school and media experience as threatening, with their new-found knowledge and ideas. None of us likes to be rejected, and the icons, language and style of youth cultures seem to say 'Adults, stay away!' There *are* barriers to entering youthful subcultures, which incarnational ministry must overcome.

Another reason stems from the Church's responsibilities to adults. Church growth does not usually begin with ministries to children and youth. It is not the intention of this chapter to make youth ministry the first and pre-eminent priority of the Church. But with all the Church is called upon to do, it cannot neglect young people.

Differences in youth ministry philosophy can also paralyse youth ministry initiatives in an 'either–or' division over strategy. Rather, we should allow the Spirit to bless a 'both–and' strategy. Some young people want discussions, celebrations and service enterprises. Others are responding to more evangelical proclamations of the Gospel. Many youth are seeking worship experiences that are more charismatic and in keeping with their music and style. If any youth ministry is true to the Scriptures, faithful to the basic tradition of the Church, safe from cultic and socially dangerous extremes and Christ-centred, it should be encouraged.

A caller to a radio talk-show was impressive. Besides being part of only 13 per cent of American parents who take care of their children full-time, he was doing so as a male spouse whose wife had a profession. 'I am taking care of two sons,' he said. 'The older is outgoing; it is as if he has always wanted to join our world. We have discovered our younger son to be slightly autistic. We have learned so much as we have been forced to sit quietly and enter his world.'[14] Once again, we are reminded about our challenge to enter the world of young people, as well as to be senstive to differences in subcultures and individuals. In such ministry there are many right ways, and we should do nothing to hinder those that are not to our particular taste.

A final obstacle to a dynamic fulfillment of Christ's Great Commission in respect to youth, is the misplacement of Church priorities. Ungodly and self-serving ecclesiastical politics, along with desire for personal status, are sure to defeat new initiatives for youth (especially since we have admitted youth ministry to be a secondary responsibility of the Church).

Adults with resources and power can press all kinds of agendas on the Church, while youth are marginalized and neglected. It is a healthy exercise to examine the content of Church concerns with young people in mind. One of St. Paul's great regrets with the early churches was what he saw as their diversionary quarrels and controversies.[15] When Jesus found his disciples embroiled in debate, he brought a child and set him in the middle of their discussion as a firm reminder about productive priorities and spirit.

We can better assess the substance of Church debates as we listen to the cries of young people.

> Honestly considering a new mandate for youth ministries leads us to conclude, not only that today's youth crisis demands such, but that the Church today desperately needs the renewal that attention to incarnational youth ministry will likely bring.

*Stories*

Stories have already come our discussion; such mention could hardly be restrained. The emphasis underlines their importance to youth ministry. Those who tell a society's stories and create its tunes will undoubtedly control that culture. Jewish culture more than most believes in stories and that God created us as story-telling and story-receiving creatures. There is no mystery about who is telling our young people stories and writing their tunes today. A half-hour of television will give a child multiple story plots and dozens of powerful commercials. All are stories. In contrast to youth in traditional societies, who had one or two good stories to process a week, young people today are barraged by stories with messages too numerous to process.

Where other social systems fail, it is the duty of the Church and youth ministry to help young people process a wide range of conflicting messages, values and beliefs. And it is our special privilege to convey to them the Great Story. Realize that these young people are developing an immunity to messages and a suspicion of story-tellers, in order to protect themselves. Yet, still they are craving to tell their own stories, because they seem trivialized in the midst of sensationalized fantasies. They yearn for real and redemptive stories. The exegesis of popular movies and music indicates their deep and unfulfilled desires. In the midst of cultures that would kill our children's stories and dreams, we must help them preserve personal and cultural histories and foster visions of hope.

'I will pour out my Spirit on all flesh . . . and your young men shall see visions.'[16] 'Where there is no vision the people perish.'[17]

Few would argue that young people today need healthy and realistic dreams, hopes and a sense of purpose. Nor that these are what the Church is meant to provide.

Young people need stories in forming their identities, and cultures are held together by stories. If the Church's story is weakened or confused, youth and society are losers. The first great missionary of the Christian Church cried out: '. . . woe to me if I do not proclaim the Gospel!'[18] The Church must decide that nothing is more important than telling that story and seeing youth ministry as a telling of stories. The story of God's love and grace outshines all other stories and, told by those they trust, is incredibly attractive to postmodern young people. The Good News embodies justice, peace and hope to secular societies searching for moral foundations.[19]

---

> If we can regain our sense of excitement and commitment about young people and the Good News they seek, there may be real hope for today and tomorrow. Considering youth ministry in terms of identity, culture and stories is the place for us, for youth leaders, and for young people themselves to begin.

---

## Notes

1. Conference Notes, Episcopal Diocese of Massachusetts, USA, 1990, quoted by Dean Borgman in *When Kumbaya Is Not Enough*, Peabody, MA: Hendrickson Publishers, 1997, p.232.
2. Adam K. A. Chepkwony, 'The Youth: A Challenge to The Church in Africa Today', *African Ecclesial Review*, Feb. 1996, Vol. 38, No. 1, p. 27.
3. *ibid*. p. 28.
4. The extremely important topic of sexuality in youth is not discussed in this paper. A theological introduction to sexuality may be found in Borgman, *op. cit.*, pp. 189–219.
5. For more of a theology of growth, see *ibid.*, pp. 89–104.
6. David Elkind, *All Grown Up and No Place To Go: Teenagers in Crisis*, Reading, MA: Addison-Wesley, 1998, p. 21 (first published 1984).
7. Further theological reflections on family and peers are in Borgman *op cit.*, pp. 105–25. For a discussion of media and music, see pp. 126–88.

8. Luke 7: 32.
9. This vital and complex topic is further discussed in Borgman, *op cit.*, pp. 62–88.
10. John 1:14a, NRSV.
11. John 20: 21b, NRSV.
12. Philippians 2: 5–8.
13. Ezekiel 22: 30, NRSV.
14. Christopher Leydon's 'The Connection' April, 1998.
15. Romans 1: 29; 14:1; 2 Corinithians 12: 20; Philippians 1: 17; 2: 3–4; Colossians 3: 13; 1 Timothy 1: 3, 4, 6; 6: 4–5; 2 Timothy 2: 24; Titus 3: 2, 9.
16. Joel 2: 28, NRSV.
17. Proverbs 29: 18, AV.
18. 1 Corinthians 9: 16b, NRSV.
19. For analysis of the Gospel and how it might be communicated to young people today, see Borgman, *op cit.*, pp.229–32; and Pete Ward's *Youthwork and the Mission of God*, London: SPCK, 1997, pp. 103–15.

# 3

# A Multitude of Voices

## Youth Ministry in Aotearoa New Zealand and Polynesia

### *Helen Wilderspin*

This is the story of one Church made up of three strands, three *tikanga* (cultures), a multitude of voices. This is not one story but many, standing with the past, the history of this land, the *tangata whenua*[1] and the *pakeha*[2] together, in the present walking towards the future.

The Anglican Church of Aotearoa New Zealand and Polynesia is inextricably bound by history, anger, forgiveness, exceptional creativity, deep soul searching and the Gospel. For the most part this is the account of a ministry forged in the wake of a visionary church, ministry to, for, with and from young people. It is written by one who stands in the *pakeha tikanga*, aware of who I am in relationship to my own *tikanga* and the *tikanga* of Maori and Polynesia, but noting that, although this story comes out of discussions and reflections with others, it is principally told from a *pakeha* perspective.

In 1992 the Anglican Church in the Province revised its constitution to reflect the partnership between *pakeha*, Maori and Polynesia. This change is evident in the new name of the Province: The Anglican Church in Aotearoa New Zealand and Polynesia. The revised constitution was based on an acceptance of the Treaty of Waitangi as the founding document of this nation and binding on the Church. The Church also sought to explore the implications of the Treaty in terms of bi-cultural development and partnership.

As applied to the church, bi-cultural development means taking steps to ensure that the Gospel of Christ takes root in, and is expressed through two different cultural forms within the one provincial or national Church. It witnesses to the enriching diversity of God's creation, and at the same time recognizes the essential unity of all creation in Christ ... Partnership involves co-operation and inter-dependence between distinct cultural or ethnic groups within one nation. It implies that Maori and Pakeha have gifts to give and receive from one another and that nationhood is best established when both partners are valued and respected and share in decision making and the resources of the nation ... the principle of partnership means that each cultural group or people is accorded the same dignity in Christ, make their distinctive contribution to the common life of the Church and each encourages and supports the other. There is mutual responsibility and inter-dependence within the Body of Christ.[3]

Since the beginning of European contact the Church has been involved in New Zealand. There was a Maori Anglican Church before the colonial or 'settler' Church was established in New Zealand. (Unfortunately the Maori Church was not mentioned in the constitution of 1857, which established the Anglican Church in New Zealand.) Missionaries from the Anglican Church were at the signing of the Treaty of Waitangi in 1840, encouraging Maori to sign it.

The Province of the Anglican Church of New Zealand also includes the islands of Polynesia. In the early 1990s, and prior to the changes in the Church's constitution, the Provincial Youth Consultation restructured itself to reflect more closely the different cultural streams within the Church. This involved formalizing the three cultural streams: Tikanga Pakeha, Tikanga Maori and Tikanga Pasifika/Polynesia. In practical terms resources are split three ways, with each partner having an equal voice in affairs affecting young people throughout the Province.

This comment from a person involved with Tikanga Pakeha highlights the changes that have taken place over the last few years:

As a Pakeha New Zealander [of European descent], I grew up in the Anglican church very ignorant of the cultural history of

our church. It wasn't until I went to the first diocesan Youth
Synod in 1982 that I discovered the strong Maori influence in
our church. Over the next few years we struggled with the
Youth Synod being bi-cultural.

This struggle was in part about the Gospel and culture.
The struggle is not new in Christendom, in the New
Testament there was argument about circumcision. However
meeting the debate in our own context brought lots of heated
arguments and pain. For me it was a time of questioning my
own beliefs and trying to get a handle on identifying the
cultural wrapping around the Gospel. Part of being Anglican
in Aotearoa New Zealand is to acknowledge that our church
has two cultural traditions within it.

Perhaps it is wrong to claim that the adult church changed
its structures because the youth did it first. However I think
the change in the Youth structure did have some influence
over the changes in the constitution. It may be a case of youth
enlightening the whole church.

Each partner has its own structure and works with youth within
their *tikanga* in their own way. The three *tikanga* come together
regularly to discuss issues that are of common concern and for
cultural exchanges, named the Tikanga Youth Exchange (TYE).
The other important area of partnership is in representation. When
our Province is asked for representation we try to make sure that it
reflects the partnership of the three *tikanga*.

One of the first international forums where the Province of
New Zealand was represented in this three *tikanga* partnership was
at the International Anglican Youth Conference in Belfast in 1988.
A comment from a member of the delegation from Tikanga
Pakeha:

> I was one of thirteen from our Province to attend the gather-
> ing. Having people from the three partners in our delegation
> strengthened our identity as a Province. Maori clergy gave a
> blessing to the whole delegation at the airport before leaving
> for Belfast. For me this blessing was significant because we
> were beginning a journey together as a delegation from New
> Zealand and Polynesia.
>
> I was proud to be part of a delegation that reflected so

well the cultural diversity of our Province. For me having different cultural traditions within our delegation added richness to the whole experience of the conference. It also reminded us who were Pakeha and the rest of the Anglican Communion that our Province had three cultural streams within the church.

I was shocked and surprised in Belfast to find that we were the only western country that included indigenous people in its delegation. While delegates from America, Canada and Australia may have referred to struggles of their indigenous people none of them had people who could speak for themselves. By modeling the three *tikanga* partnership the New Zealand/Polynesian delegation gave a challenge to youth of other western countries in the Anglican Communion to think about inclusion of indigenous people in delegations to other events.

The three *tikanga* relationship is not easy because often we talk past each other. Working across *tikanga* takes time, energy and commitment from all the partners. However the rewards of working through difficult issues are often a deeper appreciation of partnership and of the Gospel of Christ.

Tikanga Youth Exchange has been a vital part of the diverse nature of the Anglican Church in Aotearoa. Initially set up in 1986 as the Provincial Youth Consultation, the name was changed in 1994 to reflect a change in constitution and a new model of being three *tikanga* in one church.

Hosted by a different *tikanga*, TYE is held every two years, and is organized and arranged, according to their protocol, by Kawa, Tovo Vakavanua, Anga Faka Tonga and Fa'a Samoa. From a paper produced at the 1989 PYC (ratified in 1992) the following statements and principles were agreed:

The aims of Anglican Youth Ministry within the three *tikanga*: being open to see God's visions; voice of youth; searching out and doing God's will; establishing and growing a living relationship between and within each partner; providing support for youth ministry at all levels within the Province; providing a lead for our Church; [being] a place of encouragement and inspiration; youth workers getting together to share God's work in their area.

The underlying theology is taken from Galatians 3: 26–29: 'There is neither Jew nor Greek, slave nor free, male nor female – for all are one in Christ.' And Ephesians 4: 5–6: 'Our unity is not in our structures but it is in our faith ... One Lord, one faith, one baptism'.

The implications of these verses is that each individual, and each partner group equally reflect Christ; no one race or culture is more favoured or more Christian than another; while all cultures are equal, each culture is paramount in its own place and context. And we believe that the church needs to reflect these principles in its structure. The context for the last implication is the paramount importance given to Te Tiriti o Waitangi (The Treaty of Waitangi) and that it is the responsibility of the three partners, especially the Pakeha delegates to have a commitment to, prerequisite knowledge of the Treaty and the responsibilities under bi-cultural partnership and particularly a 'heart knowledge' of the Treaty.

In structural terms this means equal representation (14 delegates and 1 delegation leader for each *tikanga*) and an equal voice/vote (one vote for each partner/*tikanga* and a consensus required for any resolution to be made), for all three partners – Tikanga Maori, Tikanga Polynesia and Tikanga Pakeha.

One of the main aims of this gathering is 'that the youth of the Province of New Zealand undertake to learn about and understand each others' cultures'. A song composed by Tomasi Lino, a previous Youth Coordinator for the Diocese of Polynesia, captures the essence of Tikanga Youth Exchange:

TYE     TYE     TYE     TYE

*Malo e lelei, Namaste, Bula Vanaka,*
*Talofa, Kia Ora,* Hello my Friend.
Together we are one and praise the Lord
Say Amen for thy will be done.

The Tikanga Youth have come today,
Youths from near and far away

> All are here with something to say
> Understanding other cultures
> For a better day.
>
> Wake up, wake up, my friend today,
> Hand in hand we'll drive away
> All the wrongs of yesterday,
> That blinded our mind in many a ways.

TYE     TYE     TYE     TYE

But it is the stories of each TYE and delegates that provide the flesh, the incarnation of the TYE structure and constitutional backbone of the Church in this Province. The following are excerpts from the account of the TYE held in Samoa in 1995.

A traditional welcome was held at 2pm. The All Saints Youth presented the Ava in a dignified and competent way. It was a good introduction to Samoan life for the participants and most seemed to respect the significance even if they did not understand the words ... Participating with those from the Tikanga Polynesia were 23 young men and women from Fiji, Tonga, American Samoa and Western Samoa. This *tikanga* was joined by two from New Zealand: Tikanga Pakeha and Tikanga Maori. It was a culturally rich and colourful group who came together with a variety of goals. The primary goals being to worship God and learn from each other. After a nourishing breakfast, all people prepared for Sunday worship in All Saints Church. The service was enhanced by readings ... by the various Tikanga in their own tongue. Intercession afforded all delegates the opportunity to pray in their own language ...

After the sun had moved from its zenith, it was cool enough to do some thinking and talking. Each diocesan group met to elect representatives and discuss issues for the TYE forum. Judging by my observation there was a great deal to discuss and a lot of sharing of ideas. Temper[s] did get a little hot, and there were several participants who seemed to want to be anywhere else. Still, I reckon that it was a good experience for the younger members of the youth, and an opportunity for them to learn about TYE and the process ... In general, the meeting saw a balance of participation by each *tikanga* ...

After dinner, there was the first pair of Bible Studies led by Fr Winston ... While he spent some time in explanation and description, the majority of time was spent with *tikangas* fishing for answers to suggested questions. The questions were difficult, and my *tikanga* spent time wrestling with an honest understanding of ourselves in relation to the passage. We gathered together again to exchange answers with other *tikangas*. I was struck with the rich differences in approach to answering the questions within *tikanga*, and the presentation of these stories to others. There is a depth in the shared experience which I will remember longer than the actual study itself ...

When the *tikanga* broke into groups on this [second] day, there was a tremendous difference from the previous day. People who had never spoken publicly before, were offering even shouting suggestions. There was dialogue in different languages, and a restless energy ... I was delighted that there was no unanimous agreement, and that people felt strongly enough to maintain a position. It made a challenge for our facilitator, and the other *tikanga*, but I think that it was good for us.

From TYE in 1994 comes this Maori proverb, which is, I think, a key to the importance and continued strength of these youth exchanges:

*Ma te whakaatu ka mohio, ma te mohio ka marama, ma te marama ka matau, ma te matau ko te oranga tunutanga.*

By discussion comes understanding, by understanding comes light, by light comes wisdom, by wisdom comes everlasting life.

Yet the story of youth ministry and commitment in this country is more than a bi-annual exchange. It is also about youth ministry within each *tikanga*, the joys, triumphs, pains and disappointments. The constant searching for ways of making the Gospel relevant and heard by our various cultural strands both within the Church and the wider community. For as a Church we have a commitment to our community, our *whanau* (family), to be Christ and to find Christ where we live and in the people we live with. So the pains of our society are very close to home and affect us just as much as anybody else. So the last part of this chapter will look at the issues that concern and affect young people in this part of the world, our common life together.

The needs of Maori Anglican youth in Aotearoa are met by Te Pihopatanga O Aotearoa (the Bishopric of Aotearoa New Zealand). The Pihopatanga delivers the Anglican message to Maori in a distinctly Tikanga Maori expression, through the leadership of the Rt Revd Whakahuihui Vercoe and Pihopa Awhina (*tikanga –* convening bishop), within their own *amorangi* (the Maori equivalent of a diocese).

Working within the five Hui Amorangi is the Tikanga Maori Rangatahi (youth/young people) scene. This vibrant scene strives constantly to provide programmes which are both culturally and age appropriate – continually assisting young Maori to enter into a living relationship with the Risen Christ. The basis of these programmes are the fivefold mission statement of the worldwide Anglican Communion: to Proclaim the Good News of the Kingdom; to teach, baptize and nurture new believers; to respond to human needs by loving service; to seek to transform unjust structures of society; and to preserve the environment of the planet for future generations.

One area mentioned above, that of proclamation and evangelism is commented on in the following reflections:

> In our community of . . ., evangelism, the Word of God, the Gospels, were constantly being heard at all levels from Te Kohanga Reo [Maori language class – especially for pre-school children], through to Sunday Schools, to schools, and within the community *huihui* [gatherings]. We experience evangelism at *karakia* [prayer], day and night, daily, we live it, it is a living experience at birthdays, weddings, *tangi* [deaths/funerals], and unveilings and community gatherings. We grew up with evangelism, we were nurtured throughout our lifetimes in the faith, our *pakeke*, our *kuia* [female

elders], our Church, our *kaumatua* [elders] were good role models, as children we have been hearing the Word in our homes, within our family gatherings ... Our Nanny would *karakia* at the drop of a hat, she would lay on hands to the sick, at *tangi* or other *huihui* we would be constantly hearing familiar words, the spirit of God is ever constantly moving.

Imaginative programmes and activities, such as youth nights, camps, Bible runs, leadership training and support, *taapapa* distant education participation, inter parish exchanges and inter *amorangi* exchanges ensure that youth are active in each of the five *amorangi* of Taitokerau; Te Manawa O Te Wheke; Tairawhiti; Te Upoko O Te Ika and Te Waipounamu. Encouraging a good flow of ideas, fun and friendship between young people in the Hui Amorangi is the Kahui Rangatahi O te Pihopatanga (Youth Council), with its aims and objectives including:

• To represent our Hui Amorangi on Rangatahi issues.
• To authorize all Rangatahi initiatives and issues on a National and International level.
• To keep clear and effective communications between Maori Rangatahi and other groups such as the Hui Amorangi, Te Pihopatanga O Aotearoa, Tikanga Pakeha and Tikanga Polynesia.
• To establish Kahui Rangatahi representation on the Standing Committee of Te Runanganui [national *tikanga* council].
• To establish a Rangatahi Ministry training programme.
• To explore all funding options to meet the objectives of Kahui Rangatahi.

In Tikanga Pakeha there are also many approaches and models that are being explored by those involved in youth ministry. From an ecumenical distance education diploma in youth ministry, to something called the Comprehensive Approach, to adventure camps, art festivals and Youth Alpha, from youth groups of varying sizes and intentions, to mentoring and buddy systems with older people within the church, and contemporary multi-media worship.

What follows are a few examples within the diversity and the multitude of voices that not only make up the three *tikanga* Church but also Tikanga Pakeha.

One model that has been played around with in the Diocese of Wellington is the Riverslea Adventure Camps. The Tikanga Pakeha Diocesan Youth Co-ordinator for Wellington, Tric Malcolm, wrote in a recent article:[4]

> In our place Riverslea is both a place, that has a ministry of its own, and the word that describes the adventure camps that happen there every summer ... based on experiencing life in community and the environment and challenging personal boundaries ... birthed out of a quest to meet God in creation.
>
> Young people spend about a week in a group, of which they have chosen to be a part, with five other participants and two leaders. As a group they make decisions as to what activities they will do and how difficult they will be. The adventure sports range from white water rafting, kayaking, abseiling, rap jumping, canyoning, rock climbing, mountain biking and tramping [bushwalking]. Everything is done in the context of the group. A great amount of importance is placed on the concept of the group, both in terms of decision-making and relationship ... much of the first 36 hours is spent focusing on building good foundations for the relationships in the group ...
>
> Another focus over the last decade and a half has been the presence of the Order of Saint Francis. Each summer a couple of Brothers participate and, when available, a Sister or two have come to be with us ... They offer young people a glimpse of what 'vocation' is all about ... Many young people experience at Riverslea a living community of faith that moves through both deep joy and deep pain, 24 hours a day ...
>
> ... this piece of land speaks: it moves your soul and lets you know that God is awesome and very present. Many have likened that presence to the Wairua (spirit) or Mauri (life-force) of a Marae.[5] It is on your home Marae you are granted the right to 'stand' or to be. It is this that grounds you in knowing who you are. Young people often seek a place where they feel they belong and can feel 'at home'. The ground that makes a Marae is sacred, but a Marae is also the people, to whom it belongs. For many young people it [Riverslea] has

become their Marae – their place of belonging and their place
to stand. There is a stand of trees overlooking the river, called
the Beech Tree Grove. For many this is where the spirit is
strongest ... Often I think it is the spirit of the place that
gives the programmes the essence that makes them precious,
and keeps the energy for the future going.

A theory of Youth ministry that has been used in the last five or six
years is the Comprehensive Approach. Developed in America by
John Roberto and the Center for Ministry Development, it is an
approach that has been adapted and redesigned in Australia and
New Zealand. It is about looking at the mission and ministry of the
whole Church and ways in which young people can be an integral
part of the Church community, not just an extra bonus: a partnership of family/*whanau*, Church/secular community, educational
bodies with children and young people, 'an offering of the whole
gospel for the whole of the community'.
Examples of the type of minstry that this approach invites
include: 'All ages are involved from small children to grandparents
in helping out at a City Mission, serving food and offering
company to those living there.'[6]

A Christian Religious Education teacher, a volunteer, could
no longer cope with the rigors of classroom teaching. With
her Church's help she recruited a team of young people
available after school. With their help an after school club
provided children she had previously taught opportunity to
continue to explore the Bible's teaching and its meaning for
living. She sought the support of the school council through
the Church so that parents could be informed about her
intentions and integrity. Relationships with the children and
their parents grew, offering many opportunities to practise
the presence of God with others.[7]

Youth ministry in Tikanga Pakeha has, until recently, just gone
about its day-to-day life, fighting once a year for recognition and
funding at various diocesan synods and national forums. Going
about its own business, a sort of independent youth culture. But
recently we were encouraged at a Tikanga Pakeha National Board

47

on Ministry and Mission that we could be partners with them in our area of expertise – youth ministry. We are now an integral part of the life and ministry of the church. In addition, after a period of five years, the National Youth Network Facilitator position for Tikanga Pakeha will become a full-time position in 1999 and 2000. Moreover, five out of seven dioceses have staff employed to work in youth ministry for their dioceses.

Our challenge now is to work on our own identity as Tikanga Pakeha young people, to determine whether we have our own cultural identity separate from, and in partnership with, the rest of the *tikanga*, to stand independently, or to become fully integrated in the wider Church. And, above all, what it means for us in our secular communities to be part of a multivoiced Church of three equal partners.

Youth ministry in Tikanga Polynesia is based on a diocesan model of Archdeaconries, parishes and youth groups and the facilitation and training of the leaders within those groupings. Most of those involved in youth ministry in Tikanga Polynesia/Pasifika are based in Polynesia and the islands that exist within its boundaries, but there is an Archdeaconry in New Zealand, mainly based in Auckland.

The following are excerpts from a report made in 1997 by Jone Teana, the Diocesan Youth Co-ordinator:

> At a parish level each has its own programme to follow through the year, although most groups have similar activities, such as Bible Studies, visiting the sick and aged, those in hospital and prison, rallys, camping, fund raising, cultural nights and assisting parish practical work.
>
> At Archdeaconry level there are regular fellowships for meetings and activities vary greatly. The significant factor here is the distance between youth groups, some have only to travel by road whereas others have to brave long trips by sea. Because of this some Archdeaconries enjoy easier conditions and are able to meet quite regularly to share experiences. This is especially true for the Suva area [Fiji].
>
> And again at a diocesan level organizing a youth event over the vast area of the diocese is also not possible and it is only at events like the Tikanga Youth Exchange that a representative few can get together.

Some of the issues facing young people within the Diocese of Polynesia include a loss of direction, lack of motivation and an inconsistent spiritual life.

> In general our Youth have still not grasped the full signifi-
> cance of their contribution to the Church, the community and
> its implication to their own personal growth. The trend now
> is that virtually all over young people, due to lack of objec-
> tivity and personal goals, feel invalid and become 'drifting' in
> their communities and in their parishes. This can be attrib-
> uted to several factors such as very limited education,
> improper guidance during their childhood and cultural sensi-
> tivities . . . While all youth groups have appointed leaders, not
> all are properly equipped for the task of leadership. One thing
> stands out and that is their enthusiasm and interest. But those
> attributes are not sufficient to enable a leader to guide a
> group of young people in the midst of a rapidly changing
> world. In most cases these leaders do not have the personal
> resources to assist them to achieve their own goals. Some are
> not sufficiently educated to provide sufficient guidance yet
> they often face criticism from the uncommitted 'learned'
> ones . . .

An issue not raised in the report, but mentioned at various three-*tikanga* gatherings, is that of language. There is such a variety of languages within the one diocese that communication can often be difficult and the development of printed resources for use around the diocese complicated, expensive and time-consuming.

In the above report there were also suggestions for future development in the wake of the issues raised. Some of the areas mentioned were that the Diocese of Polynesia consider designing a youth curriculum 'that embodies important areas relevant to youth life for consistent youth training'. That leadership training be a regular feature, especially in Archdeaconries, and that it include training in the area of evangelism 'to empower the total ministry of the church'. And finally, that local project-oriented programmes be created, which would enable individuals and communities to generate income for the activities mentioned above, since many young people come from low income families.

But there are issues which are three-*tikanga*, even if sometimes they only appear to be a one-*tikanga* or two-*tikanga* concern. Some of the issues and challenges that are facing all young people include the following.

- The lack of communication between young and old, amongst the young people themselves, and between the different *tikanga* within the Church and in society.
- The difficulties within each *tikanga* of clashes between Christian ideology and cultural ideologies, especially in Tikanga Maori where Maori ideology is such a pervasive and foundational way of life.

- Youth suicide
- Sexual, emotional and physical abuse
- Abortion
- Misuse of drugs and alcohol
- Truancy in schools
- Unemployment
- Health
- Poverty and the increasing disparity between rich and poor
- The high cost of education.

In recent statistics the unemployment rate, although only 7.1 per cent overall and 5.5 per cent for Pakeha, is 18.3 per cent for Maori, and for Pacific Islanders living in New Zealand it is 16.4 per cent.[8] New Zealand recorded the fastest growing gap between rich and poor for any OECD country in the early years of this decade.[9] The New Zealand Poverty-measurement Project esti- mates that 18.5 per cent of households, containing 33 per cent of New Zealand's children, are below the poverty line. Maori are 2.5 times more likely to be in poverty than Pakeha; Pacific Island people 3.5 times more likely. Housing costs are the greatest cause of poverty.[10]

One of the most specific causes of poverty for young people of any ethnic group was the change from government-funded free tertiary education to a user pays scheme in the early 1990s. Loans were made available to cover the costs of tertiary education, but the true extent of the price paid by individuals and society is only now being recognized. The total student loan debt at 31 March

1998 was over two billion dollars, owed by 223,320 borrowers; 25,881 borrowers owed over $20,000 each, and 7,906 owed over $30,000.[11] What a way to start out in life!

Partly as a result of these staggering statistics, the General Synod (*te Hinota Whanui*) of the Anglican Church unanimously agreed on 13 May 1998 on a March or *Hikoi* of Hope from all parts of its constituency to meet in Wellington at Parliament. The March aims to demand an end to Government policies which are creating intolerable levels of poverty and social breakdown. The Bishop of Aotearoa, the Rt. Revd Whakahuihui Vercoe, said that a *Hikoi* is used to draw the attention of the public to an unjust structure and to call on the nation to join and become a unified voice, and to bring their physical presence. 'It shows you where to stand, and where you're coming from. It is a way to arouse the public mind on issues people should be united about.'[12] Full support has been offered by the young people of the Church and it is expected that many will join the March in our own areas and in significant numbers in Wellington. It will be a great opportunity to stand alongside all members of the Church and community to speak out against the unjust policies of the Government. The *Hikoi*, when it arrives in Wellington, will present the following demands: creation of real jobs; a public health system that people can trust; benefit and wage levels that move people out of poverty; affordable housing and education.

There are also other areas of hope in the Church: the development of a New Zealand Prayer Book, *He Karakia Mihinare O Aotearoa* (first published in 1989), and the continuing commitment to and challenge of *tikanga rua* relationships (relationships between two *tikanga*).

The New Zealand Prayer Book is important not just because it is indigenous in its response to the people of this Province, but also in its attempt at inclusive language and use of contemporary liturgies and poetry. There is an Eucharistic prayer in English with the parallel Maori liturgy alongside (page 476), a full Maori liturgy of the Eucharist, *He Tikanga Ano* (page 494), and the translation of the Thanksgiving of the People of God, from the Eucharistic liturgy, into Fijian and Tongan.

Important *tikanga rua* relationships include discussions amongst regional workers and young people at diocessan and Hui Amorangi level, and exchanges between Tikanga Polynesia and

51

Tikanga Pakeha in Fiji and New Zealand, and Tai Tokerau and the Archdeaconry of Polynesia in Auckland.

This short account offers a brief insight into the life and continuing story of youth ministry in the Anglican Church of Aotearoa New Zealand and Polynesia. It is a time of discovery, of challenge and commitment to a process that raises issues as fast as it addresses and solves them. I feel honoured to be a part of this dynamic, ongoing relationship, this determination to work out what it means to be Maori, Pakeha and Polynesian in the Anglican Church in this Province and in this land of Aotearoa New Zealand. To work out what it means to stand in this place, to speak, to listen and to be heard within a multitude of voices.

I'll finish with a poem/prayer from one of New Zealand's most well-known poets, James K. Baxter:[13]

> Lord, Holy Spirit,
> You blow like the wind in a thousand paddocks,
> Inside and outside the fences,
> You blow where you wish to blow.
>
> Lord, Holy Spirit,
> You are the kind fire who does not cease to burn,
> Consuming us with flames of love and peace,
> Driving us out like sparks to set the world on fire.
>
> Lord, Holy Spirit,
> In the love of friends you are building a new house,
> Heaven is with us when you are with us.
> You are singing your song in the hearts of the poor.
> Guide us, wound us, heal us. Bring us to the Father.

## Notes

1. The people of the land.
2. Term applied to native born or acculturated New Zealanders of European descent.
3. *Te Kaupapa Tikanga Rua* (Bi-cultural Development), 1986, p.34.

* The above design was created originally for a national three *tikanga* pilgrimage in 1995, with the addition of the butterfly for the 1997 Tikanga Youth Exchange, Wellington.

4. *New Trends*, Jan. 1998, pp.8–9.
5. A Marae is a traditional Maori gathering place, usually with a meetinghouse (Wharenui). It is a symbol of the people, of their tribal identity and of their belonging.
6. From a conversation at a Comprehensive Approach weekend, Auckland, March 1998.
7. From *Comprehensive Approach*, edited by Craig Mitchell, p.33.
8. *Household Labour Force Survey*, Statistics NZ, March quarter, 1998.
9. Barclay, P. *Joseph Rowntree Foundation Inquiry into Income and Wealth*, Vol.1, Joseph Rowntree Foundation, York 1995.
10. Measuring Poverty in NZ. *Social Policy Journal of NZ* (Te Puna Whakaaro), No.5.
11. Inland Revenue Dept. *Outstanding Loans Balance Report as at 31/3/98*, Wellington.
12. Hikoi of Hope briefing sheet for General Synod.
13. From 'Song of the Holy Spirit', verses 1, 5 and 6.

* The above design was made during the 1994 Tikanga Youth Exchange, Rotorua.

# 4

# Palestinian Young People in the Anglican Church

## *Yazeed Said*

As I start to think of the young people in Israel/Palestine, I cannot but think of the whole people. For there is not and there cannot be a divorce between the study of the Palestinian people, and the story of the young Palestinian people, Anglican and others, regardless of their religion, or Church affiliation. In this short study I will try to show, rather briefly, how the story and the history of the Palestinian people at large affected, and still affects, Palestinian Anglicans – specifically those of the young generation.

Palestinians, and among them Palestinian Christians, have roots which strike deep in the land and society of Palestine. They are an indigenous group, some of whom trace their descent from the early Church, while others trace it from the events and historical developments which made modern Palestine what it is. Worldwide, Palestinian Christians number 400,000, or 6.7 per cent of a total Palestinian population of six million. 51,000 of these 400,000 Palestinian Christians live in the West Bank and Gaza, while there are 114,000 Palestinian Christians in Israel. The indigenous Christian population of the Holy Land numbers 165,000, 41.5 per cent of all Palestinian Christians worldwide. The Christians of the West Bank and the Gaza Strip are only 2.9 per cent of the entire Palestinian population in the Occupied Territories.

Palestinian Christians contribute far more to the national community than their numbers would at first suggest. In part their contribution is tied to the relatively high level of education, and to their preference for liberal professions and white collar occupations.

The Palestinian Christians, as all Palestinians are, are part of the wider context of Arab Christianity, which refers to those who profess the Christian faith in the Arabic language of the several Eastern Christian communities in the Middle East. For the most part, it also embodies the expression of Christian life and thought in the world of Islam, where Arabic is not only the language of daily life, but the *lingua sacra* of the dominant Islamic culture of the Arab region. The discussion of 'Arab Christianity', therefore, neatly falls under two headings: 'Before the Rise of Islam' and 'The World of Islam'. In both categories, the Arab Christians received the basic formulations of their faith from other languages, principally Greek, Syriac and Coptic. So Arab Christianity is, in an initial way, a Christianity in translation. But, over the centuries it has found its own distinctive voice, and thus it has a major contribution to make to the wider Christian world, especially wherever Christians live in harmony with Muslims.

Christians in the Middle East used to be the majority, especially in the northern parts of the Middle East, until after the time of the Crusades, when the numbers of Christians in the Arab world steadily declined; under the Ottomans they were well in the minority in the general population. By the 20th century, many communities had already forged a relationship with one or more of the great colonial powers, who afforded them a measure of protection and, often, a certain economic advantage, which offered greater access to the burgeoning culture of the West than most Muslims enjoyed. At the same time, however, Christian groups from the West, Catholic and Protestant alike, made inroads into the Arab Christian communities under the aegis of the colonial powers, and through their missionary activities brought further divisions to an already splintered Christian population. Nevertheless, it was largely Christian thinkers and writers in the first half of this century who launched the Arab Nationalism movement that has dominated the politics of much of the Middle East in the second third of the 20th century. Similarly, Christians were prominent in the arts, and in the educational and business enterprises of the Arab world. But, by the last third of the century, with the rise of what the West calls 'Islamic Fundamentalism', Christian populations in the Middle East and North Africa were on the wane again. Emigration to the West has, in fact, all but completely depleted their ranks in areas where formerly they were strong.

In Europe and North America, immigrant Arab Christians readily accommodated themselves to the culture of their host countries. And for many of them Arabic itself is lost by the second generation. It survives in Church services but, for the most part, the Arab Christian identity is lost in favour of the old denominational loyalties, which in Arab lands had always been modified by membership of the larger Arab culture.

The national identity of Palestinian Christians is rooted in the same experience which befell the entire Palestinian society. In 1948, as a result of the creation of the State of Israel, over 714,000 Palestinians became refugees: 7 per cent, or 50,000 of these refugees were Christian, and they made up 35 per cent of all Christians who lived in Palestine prior to 15 May, 1948.

At present, Palestinian Christians have undergone the same measures and processes which arise from the occupation. However, there is a distinction which must be made and realized between Palestinians in Israel and those living in what is known in the West as the West Bank and Gaza Strip, preferably called Palestine. Until very recently, the *Intifada,* as a popular uprising, saw Christians and Muslims engaged in an effort to end the occupation and achieve independence. The records of young Christians imprisoned and martyred are other indications of the attachment to, and identity with, Palestine and its cause. In addition, the active involvement and participation of Palestinian Christians in all aspects of life in the country is itself a testimony to the love they harbour for their country and their fellow Palestinians.

Young Palestinians in Israel fall into a different context and, indeed, complex. For they are part of the historic continuity of the indigenous people of Palestine, but happen to be in the modern State of Israel, because their part of the land simply happened to be occupied by the newly-established State in 1948, leaving the West Bank and Gaza out. Thus, they were and are exposed to a different type of living and life, mostly influenced by the West via the New Jewish State – which is secular and Western in its essence. Young Anglicans are also part of this puzzle. With them, the matter becomes yet more complex. For if one searches for their identity, it appears too difficult to trace. They would be considered to be Israelis, by citizenship, and Palestinians, historically; yet they are also Arabs, as part of a larger Arabic speaking world, and Anglicans, most of whom today were born into Anglican families who may have converted in the past from other indigenous churches.

As a result of all this dilemma of identity and the ongoing political difficulties in the country and the region, ever since the establishment of the State of Israel, young Anglicans (and Christians at large) find it easier to find themselves in a Western country. Therefore, many of the young people go abroad to study and never return. In that manner, they continue the ongoing stream of emmigration, which began in the last century. This is true for Christians living in Israel and in the Occupied Territories of Palestine. The future, for them, looks dim in the country, but prosperous in the West.

This also reflects the difficulties that they face at home in raising new families and in seeking better education. The political situation, indeed, affects all sides and aspects of life. Not all families are fortunate enough to be able to afford their children an acceptable standard of living and education. The Church, on the other hand, is unable to reach out to help each and every child.

All of this means that young people and others, Anglican and non-Anglican, leave the Church, either by going abroad, or by neglecting it locally. Palestine, like many other countries of the East, is not exempt from the phenomenon of Westernization, which has caused the total divorce between religious life and secular life. Materialism becomes an essential habit of daily life. The Church, thus, becomes marginal and only for those who would be considered 'religious'.

The Church, in the middle of all this trauma, does not find it easy to work and help out the Christian community to live out to their different vocations. It has always been noted that the Church should train people to specialize in different areas and professions, equipping young people to bring them back to the fold. But, it is not as easy as it sounds, and the general situation in the country does not help very much.

I believe, personally, that there is a more essential task that the Church should try to accomplish, which is true in other parts of the world as well, including here in England. The Church has not been very successful in providing a kind of theological thesis and understanding of life that relates to all aspects of living. The young people want to enjoy their age and their life; indeed they deserve this. However, the Church ought to help these people understand that God is a reality and not an abstraction. It is the reality in whom we live and move and exist. There cannot be a divorce between the reality of God and the reality of humanity. The West has been very successful in thinking it has made this distinction between God and the world, but this distinction cannot exist. How do we help our people to realize this reality? Well, we don't. The reality of God is there, here and now. The ministry of the Church, I believe, ought to provide a kind of, what I would call a ministry of being and supporting the people, in all aspects and manners of life. The local Church, in other words, has to try and articulate a modern Christian theology in Arabic, well-attuned to the challenges of the age and of other faiths, and easily intelligible in the Churches in which the people live.

FURTHER READING

1. *Christians in the Holy Land*, eds Michael Prior and William Taylor, World of Islam Festival Trust, 1994.
2. Betts, R.B., *Christians in the Arab East: a Political Study*, John Knox Press, 1978.
3. Cragg, K., *The Arab Christian: A history in the Middle East*, 1991.

# 5

# Youth Ministry and Justice

*Sheryl A. Kujawa* *

At the most basic level, justice is understood as giving each person
the fundamental right of living a fully human life. The centrality of
justice to Christian life has long been recognized. Scholastic
theologians saw justice as one of the 'cardinal virtues' on which all
of the Christian life turned.[1] In more contemporary terms, justice
can be viewed as the cornerstone of true Christian community, as
the 'connective tissue' that holds together the Christian life. 'To
survive and thrive a little we need justice like a body needs blood.'[2]

In biblical thought, the litmus test for any society consists in the
way it treats widows and orphans – in short, the poor – in its midst.
Jesus taught that the poor belong to God, and that to meet the poor
is to meet Christ. Basic justice within the Church and society
demands a minimum level of participation in the life of the human
society for all people, enabling them to share in and contribute to
the common good. We are all made in the likeness of a God who
invites us to share in the creative and redemptive work of Jesus
Christ to 'recreate' the earth. The option for the poor, therefore, is
not intended to pit one marginalized group against another. Rather,
it affirms that our very salvation is dependent upon one another;
the deprivation and the powerlessness of the poor wounds the
entire community. The extent of the suffering of the poor and
marginalized is a measure of how far we are from becoming a true
Christian community.

Just as justice and community life are closely related within the
Christian tradition, so is youth ministry a ministry of justice. Youth
ministry is a justice ministry within the community of faith –

ministry to and with the young people in our midst and to the wider society – reaching out to serve youth in our society. While the more common experience of youth ministry has emphasized ministry *within* the Church community, youth ministry must also address the social situation and needs of *all* young people. A balance must be found between ministry within the Christian community, and ministry by the Christian community, to young people within our societies and world.

Further, an underdeveloped but increasingly important focus of youth ministry is the empowerment of young people to become aware of the social responsibilities of the Christian faith, found in our common call to live and work for justice and peace. Integral to any sense of justice is an awareness of the connections between justice and basic human needs. All people, including young people, have the basic right to the security of economic rights such as food, clothing, shelter and work. Every human being has the right to have their personhood valued and affirmed and to shape their own destinies. Lastly, each person has the right and duty to promote these rights with and for others.[3] Meeting essential human needs is not charity or heroic gesture; it is a minimal manifestation of our humanness. In this way, youth ministry also needs to empower young people with the knowledge and skills to transform the unjust structures of society that oppress them, so that these structures are further challenged to respect the dignity of every human being.

A more comprehensive model of youth ministry with a focus on justice suggests a contextual approach. That is, the assertion that in all places youth ministry occurs within a given social, cultural and religious context, which shapes the specific ministry. This approach takes seriously the impact of a number of social systems on young people's growth, values and faith, rather than focusing on isolated individuals. Like all Christians, young people not only exist in the world, but also relate to it and are responsible for it. Everyone exists within a series of systems. Individuals, families, governments, institutions, societies, etc. are all in a field of social interaction. Among the systems that affect young people are the family, society, the dominant culture, youth culture, racial and ethnic culture, education and the local Church community. A communal spirituality suggests that individuals are more determined by systems than by individual will. A systems approach to youth ministry asserts that every personal, social and cultural being stands in need of ongoing transformation. No human (or other form) is ever perfect, ever wholly divine. We must be ever-vigilant to evaluate critically that which we have become – comfortable and familiar.

Under the best circumstances, the Church is called to maintain a balance between the need to pass on our Anglican heritage and ancient traditions to young people, remaining open to their contributions and influences, while at the same time considering their needs as human beings made in the image of God. What does this analysis tell us about the type of youth ministry we need to consider at the end of the 20th century? It suggests the need for a major transformation – a conversion of sorts – in the way we look at our mission and ministry to and with young people. I use the word 'conversion' quite deliberately, for it suggests a profound change from one way of doing ministry to another. Genuine conversion requires an abandonment of an unsatisfying perspective in favour of a renewed sense of more meaningful life. While, in many quarters, we have successfully ministered to and with young people in the past, the evidence shows that we are still a long way from creating faith communities where young people are valued for who they are, even if that identity may threaten institutional life.

Moreover, even stronger evidence suggests that our faith communities contribute little to young people who are not already known to us, or who are significantly endangered. Whether or not our societies value young people, we have seen that the Gospel mandates that something more should be expected of the followers of Jesus, joined together in a covenanted community. Are we willing to face the fears that prevent us from becoming the kind of Church that would be more meaningful for young people, and perhaps for ourselves? Do we even want to hear what God has revealed to young people?

As part of the process of conversion towards a more complete vision of youth ministry rooted in justice, we are called to 'refound' the Church around a radical call to Gospel living, to both personal and social conversion, to moving into the world in action. Part of this move into the world, in regard to young people, is the recognition that they are who they are because they have inherited the world from earlier generations, who, far too often, have treated them with neglect, abuse, racism, sexism, addiction and other forms of oppression. As Christians we need to repent for our complicity in the factors that have and continue to devalue young people in our Church and societies.

The sad reality is that the needs of young people at every economic level get lost within the larger society, and they are then often blamed for their lack of a healthy outlook. More than ever before, national, community and religious leadership must be held responsible for assisting young people enter a society that offers genuine equality for all young people, including young people of colour, young women and the economically disadvantaged. Rich or poor, young people are in danger of turning to drugs, alcohol or suicide in an attempt to escape from the depression, self-doubt and anxiety that accompanies an uncertain future. Gay and lesbian young people, who often feel alienated and judged by the Church, have an even higher suicide rate than do heterosexual young people. Yet many of our congregations would see these endangered young people as outside their membership.

Young people are interested in knowing Jesus Christ. They are looking for identity, affirmation, healing, authenticity and community from the Church. They want to respond to a Church that has something to say about issues of importance to them – spirituality, economics, racism, violence, sexuality – perhaps even admitting our own ignorance in the face of the world's problems. Once again, we are called to stretch the boundaries of relational youth ministry to include three inter-related processes inherited from the Christian social justice tradition: liberation, evangelization and conscientization and praxis.

## Liberation

At the very core of liberation theology is the original New Testament story of the Christian movement: how the socially downcast found an alternative to life in the world that was not imagined possible. In the new Christian community all were welcome with reverence and respect. People of diverse backgrounds, histories and heritages could now begin to share together in the common story of Jesus Christ. Jesus invited all to join in a new reality that truly revolutionized the way his followers experienced themselves, their community and God. Early Christians came together not to argue or defend, but simply to sing of joy, to tell the story of Jesus, to see how they could help one another, and to celebrate the breaking of the bread.

This vision of community speaks to the kind of religious community sought by young people today. Many young people today are not only spiritually uprooted, but live in very troubled societies. Grave patterns concerning the future of humankind weigh on their hearts and minds, and they are often left feeling quite desperate. Obviously, not all young people share the same attitudes, yet current studies of this generation suggest some important characteristics for consideration when studying youth ministry.

These characteristics include, but are not limited to, the following.

- Pain. Close to 50 per cent of young people between the ages of 18 and 30 come from divorced and blended families. Many lacked a reliable adult presence while growing up. The pain experienced in family life has contributed to feeling of loneliness and isolation. For many, friends are more family than family. The search for intimacy is a driving force in the lives of these young people, who place a high value on community – meaning secure, open and inclusive relationships.
- Distrust of authority. Young people often place a higher value on personal relationships than on institutions, on authenticity rather than on excellence. It is hard to think of a form of authority that has not in some way failed young people – families, governments, educational systems, health and welfare systems, the Church. Consequently, young people tend to distrust more traditional forms of authority. In terms of the Church, denominational loyalties are becoming a thing of the past. Rather, young people are attracted to those communities where they feel valued and authenticated.
- Fear. Though young people often lead courageous lives in the face of adversity, many live in fear of what the future may bring. Young people want to find a sense of hope on a local scale and want their lives to make a difference; factors such as limited economic potential, and a ruined environment, limit their optimism. Without the potential to make it 'big' as had the previous generation, young people often seek to do good when it is achievable, in relationships and in local causes.

- Spiritual hunger. Though often ignored by organized religion, many young people are looking for transcendent meaning. Popular opinion that suggests that young people are not interested in the spiritual life, misrepresents the deep yearnings on the part of young people which are unsatisfied by traditional religion. The pastoral problem is not so much that young people do not have spiritual questions, it is that they look for the answers in all kinds of places. Not tied to denominational loyalties, young people are open to spiritual experiences that meet their needs for intimacy and community, and which are connected to larger global issues. An ever-increasing number of young people, like their older counterparts, wander to esoteric groups or sects in search of the meaning in their lives. There are presently over eight hundred such groups in North America alone.[4] Yet to young people, a Church that worships the God of holiness, of justice and rightness, of mercy and compassion is far from irrelevant. Religious leaders honestly committed to making sacrifices in the name of love are those most likely to be respected by young people.[5]

Theologically, the concept of liberation is crucial to any youth ministry that takes justice seriously. On the most basic level, liberation emphasizes the human response to the offer of salvation in Jesus Christ, and to His call to justice and peace. Liberation requires both personal and social conversion.[6] It invites young people to embody a lifestyle of Christian participation in efforts to transform and humanize the world.

Important to the discipline of youth ministry is the bringing together of liberation and education expressed by the Brazilian educator Paulo Freire, in the classic *Pedagogy of the Oppressed*. In his works Freire condemned 'banking' models of education – placing didactic information in an object's head until the time for a withdrawal – and advocated a 'dialogical' education. Dialogical education presupposes that every human person has a vocation to be a 'subject' and not the object of their own lives.[7]

Paulo Freire did not claim to be a theologian in the traditional sense of the term, but, as a committed Christian, he believed that theology has a vital role to perform as an agent of liberation in the world. Freire made an important contribution to the Church in the way he integrated his own faith into education for liberation. Just as he believed that education was never neutral, Freire believed that the political partiality, or non-neutrality of the Church should never be underestimated. He believed that the true Christian could never naively accept a Church allied with oppression. Such a stance suppresses the prophetic mission of the Church in the world and its call for justice and peace. Freire argued for an affirmation of the Church's prophetic ministry: the end of injustice and the beginning of a better world for all people.

Liberation is a significant theological theme of this century, for many it is the most significant – women, people of colour, the specially-abled, gay and lesbian people, the economically disadvantaged – many people, young and old, have declared to government, military, business, educational and religious institutions that their complicity with oppression and toleration of their lesser status is over.

At the same time, models of leadership from liberation theologians offer new visions for the Christian community that are applicable to youth ministry. Leadership has everything to do with community and youth ministry, since, at the most basic level, leadership involves the ability to evoke and empower the leadership of others. These models, often drawn from feminist sources, draw their models of leadership from a partnership paradigm. The mission of the Church is defined in this paradigm as intimately related to the search for justice, and the model of ministry is based in partnership, rather than rigid hierarchy.

This liberation-based leadership paradigm has a variety of designations, including partnership, mutuality, friendship, community. This perspective on leadership suggests a shared authority within community. Such leaders are not only interested in the reversal of the paradigm of domination, but are also looking for ways of exercising authority that are less harmful to human beings and to all of creation. Here leadership is exercised by standing in solidarity with others: power and authority are shared rather than accumulated. These leaders encourage the leadership ability of others, in particular those at the margins who do not see themselves as leaders. Its criterion of effectiveness is determined by how well leadership empowers those typically on the margins due to systemic oppression, such as racism, sexism, heterosexism, classism, disableism and the like. Clearly, such leadership models are easily adaptable to young people, particularly since the range of systemic oppressions affects them to a greater degree than their older adult counterparts. Equally clear is the appropriateness to youth ministry of examples of leadership in which authority is exercised as standing with the community in solidarity with those who are marginalized.[8]

A dialogical reading of liberation theology from the perspective of youth ministry highlights the significance of that theological movement in several ways. First, it affirms the importance of worship, community and mission for both youth ministry and for the Church itself. Second, it raises the importance of standing in solidarity with the marginalized, or with young people in the case of youth ministry, with a commitment to confront injustice. Third, it emphasizes the importance of multifaceted religious conversion for young people and older adults, as well as the Church as a whole, as part of the struggle for justice. Fourth, the perspective of liberation theology holds up a vision of the Church as a base community with a bias for the alienated, the poor and oppressed, the marginalized and the stranger. In regard to youth ministry, this perspective calls us not only to a new relationship with the young people in our midst, but to a broader vision of reaching out to the most marginalized young people in our societies.

## Evangelization

At the beginning of this century the ecumenical movement called for 'the evangelization of the world in this generation'.[9] As we stand on the threshold of the 21st century, it appears that our forebears failed to meet their goal, and we are left wondering what to do next. The need for the evangelization of young people – meaning the lifelong process of conversion whereby Christians make a personal and communal commitment to Christ and the Gospel mission of bringing about the reign of God – is inextricably linked to any theology of youth ministry seriously concerned with justice. The influence of liberation theology redefines Christian faith in terms of evangelization for the reign of God in all divisions of human life in the world. Genuine evangelization of young people is not a programme; rather it is more of an invitation and a mission. It requires leadership that has both a fervour for the Christian faith and a commitment to reach out to young people.

A major issue that youth ministers today must face is the reality that not only are there large numbers of unchurched young people, but that we must also reach large numbers of baptized, unevangelized Christians. Many young people may have received a basic religious education, but have not experienced personal conversion, nor embraced the call to live the radical life of the Gospel. Dynamic, engaging youth evangelization is often one of the most neglected areas of ministry with young people. The essential goal of this effort is to make the person and the message of Jesus Christ attractive and relevant to young people. Jim Rayburn, the founder of Young Life, a worldwide para-church organization, is often quoted as saying that it is a sin to bore young people with the Gospel.[10] Rayburn believed that Jesus Christ is so attractive that any young person who had a genuine spiritual encounter with Him would respond enthusiastically. Youth ministers ought to be equally convinced that this can be the case with young people in our communities too.

For young people, the century ahead is likely to be filled with stark realities not even considered a century ago, presenting difficult challenges for the Christian Church. The Christian hegemony of our ancestors is now called into question in many places throughout the world. Those of us who live in societies who have marginalized religion to a greater extent, need to begin to go beyond the mindset of merely replacing our decreasing numbers, and to reform and revitalize our vocation to reflect the Gospel anew.

Lately much is made by writers on youth culture of the impact of postmodern culture. Put simply, our societies are in the throes of a major transition, or the movement from modernity to postmodernity. Postmodernism is characterized by the breakdown in order as established by cultural, scientific and religious traditions. In the postmodern world, people have rejected the Enlightenment ideals of optimism and progress, replacing them with a gnawing pessimism. For the first time in generations many young people in Western societies no longer believe that progress is inevitable and that we can solve the world's problems. Their world is constantly changing, their internal life is often fragmented, and perhaps the most sobering reality is that they have adjusted to life in a state of chaos. As they confront their own downward mobility, young people are critical of the competitive lifestyles of those of us in the generations before them. Experience has taught many young people about the fragility of the human condition and the need for cooperation in order to survive.

It would be tragic if we, as Anglican Christians, ended up being among the last defenders of a dying modernity, rather than looking seriously at the issues raised by the evangelization of young people at the advent of the postmodern age, and what they mean for us. Though few suggest that we go back to the pre-scientific age, we need to come to terms with the fact that our society is no longer distinctively Christian.

In *The Culture of Disbelief*, Stephen Carter describes the people who believe in God today as a 'cultural minority'. Though this cultural minority is not numerical – polls suggest that within the United States 96 per cent profess to believe in God – it is a minority, nonetheless, because it operates silently within the culture.[11] A major part of the challenge in communicating the faith in the post-modern world is that it can all to easily become just one more piece of information available to young people already overloaded with information.[12] The legacy of this disbelief for young people is that they become adults in a culture that refuses to take religion and personal faith seriously. As author Dieter Zander comments: 'Perhaps no other generation has needed the church so much, yet sought it so little.'[13] Zander's comments are confirmed by one young woman in her mid-twenties, as she noted:

> I, for one, had a hard time trusting anything: Love is forever (my parents divorced when I was four). Uncle Sam is your friend (if you're American, and sometimes even not then). Technology will solve the world's problems (just turn off the TV, dear, and take your Prozac) ... I had no mentors in the faith. There are no Christians within climbing distance of my family tree. When I came to God, I came out of desperation.[14]

Those concerned with the evangelization of young people differ about whether the proclamation of the Gospel should be implicit or explicit. Regardless of this difference, however, it can be said that the most effective evangelists with young people are those who take seriously their lives, their cultural context and their concerns. While many approach the evangelization of young people almost solely in terms of their absence from our congregations, a more helpful approach starts out with the needs and concerns of young people themselves. Instead of asking why young people do not come to our churches, we should begin to concentrate on the question, 'How can we as a Church better respond to young people?'

Though several faith-development experts have suggested that many young people make their faith commitment by the age of 18, ironically, at the same point in their lives, our greying congregations begin to lose interest in them. There is a deep ambiguity within the institutional Church about young people which calls into question not only our sincerity about youth evangelization, but also our commitment to justice for all. However, effective youth ministry does not necessitate the abandonment of our faith communities. Rather, we need to make an effort to connect young people's experience with the community's understanding of God and the Church as a supportive community. When asked what led them to Christ, many young people will recall individuals or a community who were there when they needed them. The Gospel message is given its power when witnessed by people in a trusting relationship. As Henri Nouwen wrote:

> Ministry means the ongoing attempt to put one's own search
> for God, with all the moments of pain, joy, despair, and hope,
> at the disposal of those who want to join this search but do
> not know how.[15]

Young people are seeking personal commitment. Commitment includes a passion for justice that embraces other people, ideas, beliefs and causes. The Church is called to assist young people as they begin this formation process of building a sense of purpose and commitment in their lives. Through participation in worship and community service in the life of the Church, it can provide a focus for the curiosity, idealism and desire for commitment that is characteristic of youth. Unchurched and unevangelized young people are painfully aware that they want something more. They yearn for mentors. They yearn for a community with integrity. In a sense, they call the Church to account. They would like our faith communities to be better, to be places where a commitment to freedom, mutual direction and action are the norm.

One of the reasons meaningful worship is so important to young people today is that it is both a sign of community transformation and a vehicle for their own transformation. Young people seek a connection with the rites of the community. The problem is that so many of our communities have isolated liturgy from Christian social action, resulting in what is perceived by young people to be empty ritual and formalism. Who can take seriously a God who is detached from poverty, violence and oppression? Liturgy that responds to young people calls them to a greater sense of engagement with the world, and opens up the liturgical assembly so that they become more than spectators. Worship then becomes an extension of a vibrant inner life rather than the result of obligation or guilt.

The mystery of the Incarnation, a foundation for youth ministry and, indeed, all ministry, is evidence that God chooses to participate in the entirety of our humanity. Similarly, evangelization seeks to involve the whole of young people's experience, by opening them to God's grace in the spiritual, emotional, intellectual, volitional and socio-political dimensions of their lives. Like all of us, young people need to make sense of their lives and, deep down, are searching for meaning and purpose. But they look elsewhere than to the Church for that meaning and purpose. Why?

There are many reasons, of course, why young people today are choosing to root their identity outside the Church, and in particular the lack of meaningful supportive relationships for them within our faith communities. Evangelization is about reaching out, creating genuine bonds of friendship with young people. It's about respecting the social locations and cultural ethos of young people. It's about learning from them as well as sharing with them. Evangelization is about putting young people in touch with each other, individually and through the local organization of groups. It's about working with young people in activities for justice and peace. On the most basic level, it's about revealing the Good News of Jesus Christ through our deeds and the quality of our relationships. To evangelize young people is to instill in them confidence in the God who lives among them.

## Conscientization and Praxis

There are important connections between the evangelization of young people and critical reflection in light of the Gospel and the life of discipleship – or conscientization and praxis. The perspective of liberation theology makes clear the necessity of conscientization and praxis for the building of genuine Christian community with young people. Within this understanding of youth ministry, Christian spirituality is necessarily communal in nature, centred in the collective life of the Church, pluralistic in its expression and oriented towards service to others.[16]

Conscientization is the process whereby young people begin to reflect critically on the socio-political, cultural, economic and religious aspects of their lives and, at the same time, begin to experience themselves as agents of action in the world and acquire a commitment to change those things which go against the dignity of every human being. Only through conscientization does the Gospel become so deeply ingrained within young people that they develop a spirituality which relates to their social location and personal vocation. Here they begin to see themselves as protagonists of their own lives, claim their personal and collective histories in the present and in the future, and learn to recognize the presence of God in their own lives and in the lives of others. Moreover, conscientization is crucial to any approach to youth ministry from the perspective of justice. Without a critical consciousness young people are unable to identify the situations and structures that oppress them and that are out of step with the Gospel message. Linked with critical consciousness is Christian praxis, which involves young people, along with those of other ages, engaging in the life of discipleship in the world.

Christian conscientization and praxis enable young people to develop the skills to act freely for the liberation of themselves and others. Youth ministry rooted in justice challenges young people to go beyond spirituality for the purposes of nurturance only, to a more prophetic spirituality. The aim is to help young people pass from the mentality of religious consumer to that of co-responsibility. It challenges them to discover their own call and charisms and accept their share in the mission of the Church for the reign of God as being part of discipleship. Authentic Christian spirituality springs from discipleship and our attempts to live out a Christian praxis. Ministry with young people demands the development of profound spiritualities, not superficial slogans. They are looking for signs of transformation in those who would claim to live as Christians.

Young people do not exist solely to become well-adjusted adults.

We commit an injustice against young people if we limit their spiritual development to personal conversion. A justice perspective on youth ministry suggests that young people have a vocation in the world that is inspired by the Gospel and results in social conversion. Young people thus inspired are enabled to make use of their God-given gifts, express and share their faith, and question cultural values contrary to the Gospel. Social conversion urges young people to work for the transformation of the situations that dehumanize themselves and others, to confront difficulties courageously and to engage in society productively.[17]

## Youth Ministry and Justice

How then would youth ministry look if we took seriously the need for justice? How do we create an environment where young people are respected, valued and treated with dignity? How do we reach out to young people who are powerless, voiceless and hurting? How do we welcome them, as created in the image of God, fully into Church life, even when they challenge and disturb us? What would have to occur before young people could experience the love of Christ and His call to justice, love and peace? How would we go about guiding young people to a personal and social conversion, leading to the transformation of social institutions and structures?

Some of the signs of youth ministry from the perspective of justice are the following:

- Accepting young people as they are, helping them experience themselves as children of God and disciples of Jesus Christ.
- Developing a lasting sense of compassion for young people. Rather than treating youth as 'the other', the Church can and should, through relationships in the community foster a sense of compassion for all young people.
- Commitment to intercultural awareness and the eradication of all forms of oppression that rob young people of their God-given dignity and potential.
- Openness to a fresh understanding of age-old biblical truths in light of contemporary life.
- Contact with other Christian denominations and faith groups.
- Seeking out young people traditionally considered outside Church boundaries.

- Considering change and conflict healthy, along with the ability to discus controversial issues.
- Facilitating conscientization, helping young people embrace their vocation to be agents of action in the world.
- Encouraging local communities of young people – in dioceses, congregations, colleges, universities and social settings – that make the Gospel real by focusing on young people's needs for healthy relationships and justice.
- Building relationships with young people that encourage inter-generational dialogue and respect.
- Advocating structural and social changes within Church and societal institutions.
- Modelling community through open dialogue, Christian solidarity, mutual support, service and a sense of shared responsibility.
- Structuring worship in ways that are relevant to young people.
- Praying for young people.

For the Church to be converted to justice for young people we will need to meet the challenges of a prophetic ministry that embodies community, practises a stewardship of care, honours the politics of diversity and inclusion, and reveres mystery with a profound sense of servant ministry. All ministry, certainly all ministry with young people, is profoundly relational and is inextricably concerned with justice. No programme or liturgy will meet the needs of young people until we begin to share life authentically with them. Our life and ministry need to extend beyond Sunday mornings and parochial buildings. Instead, youth ministry can and should become a radical ministry of outreach. To do so, our Churches need to become symbols of involvement and transformation, rather than far too often symbols of legalism and exclusivity. Just as the life and ministry of the earliest Christians was not limited to the congregation, so we are called now to expand our institutional boundaries to young people who are separated from us and from one another. We owe it to young people to enable them to become active participants in bringing forth the reign of God. We owe it to the Church of the 21st century to know young people and to pass on the Gospel and the richness of its ancient traditions to them.

## Notes

* Contextual social analysis is an important part of all theological reflection; this is especially true when the primary perspective is that of liberation theology. As a theologian I believe that it is important to state clearly that I am approaching youth ministry and justice from my own perspective. That is, from the context of an ordained, middle-class, heterosexual woman of European descent from the United States. While I believe that the major arguments of this paper are appropriate to the study of youth ministry elsewhere in the world, my own context necessarily is the basis of my perspective.

1. Thomas Bright and John Roberto, *Justice*, 10.
2. Daniel C. Maguire, 'A Theory of Justice', *Justice*, 11.
3. Adapted from James McGinnis, 'Four Components of Justice', *Justice*, 15.
4. Francoise Darcy-Berube, *Religious Education At a Crossroads: Moving On in the Freedom of the Spirit*, Paulist, 1995, p.80.
5. Adapted and expanded from Sheryl A. Kujawa, 'Disorganized Religion', *Disorganized Religion: The Evangelization of Youth and Young Adults*, Cowley, 1998, pp.232–33.
6. Definition based on Prophets of Hope, *Evangelization of Hispanic Young People*, Saint Mary's Press, 1995, p.266.
7. Paulo Freire, *Pedagogy of the Oppressed*, Herder & Herder, 1970. See also his *Education for Critical Consciousness*, Seabury, 1973. For a recent analysis of Freire's contribution, see Maria Harris, *Proclaim Jubilee! A Spirituality for the Twenty-First Century*, Westminster, 1996, pp.5–7.
8. For example, Letty Russell, 'A Quest for New Styles of Ministry', *Sewanee Theological Review*, 35, 4, 1992, 344–54.
9. David Devadas, *Ecumenism and Youth* Geneva, World Council of Churches, 1995, pp.1–2.
10. Quoted in Daniel Ponsetto, *Walking Together: Outreach and Evangelization Resources for Youth Ministry*, Saint Mary's Press, 1995, p.12.
11. Stephen Carter, *The Culture of Disbelief*, New York, Basic Books, 1993, p.279.
12. Dean Borgman, *When Kumbaya is Not Enough: A Practical Theology of Youth Ministry*, Hendrickson, 1997, p.28.
13. Dieter Zander, 'The Gospel for Generation X: Making Room in the Church for Busters', *Leadership* Spring, 1995, 37.
14. Piper Lowell, 'Out of Desperation', *Sojourners* November, 1994, 20.
15. Henri J. M. Nouwen, *Creative Ministry*, Doubleday, 1971, p.111.
16. Prophets of Hope, *Evangelization of Hispanic Young People*, p.96.
17. Prophets of Hope, *Evangelization of Hispanic Young People*, pp.99–104.

# 6

# An Apostle for Youth

## *Lindsay Urwin OGS*

Although most younger clergy find it hard to believe that a bishop has lived in anything other than a largish house, enjoying all the perceived benefits of an episcopal lifestyle, the truth is that, like every other priest, the bishop too can generally trace his style and approach to ministry to experiences and incidents during the early years of his ordained life.

I was a curate in the early 1980s near the Elephant and Castle, a heavily populated area of inner-city South London. From the flat roof of the block of flats in which I lived I could just see Big Ben, and hear it if the wind was blowing in my direction. Most times, the overpowering smell of hamburgers from the burgerbar downstairs dominated any time spent in solitude on that rooftop, away from the buzz of the Walworth Road and the East Street market. Its convenient location meant that my flat was a handy resting place when the burgerbar closed at 11 p.m. and the local lads needed somewhere to chill out or devour their takeaway.

At that time unemployment among young people was rife, and many 17 to 20 year-olds had never experienced earning a wage, save for a few pounds cash-in-hand on a market stall. I discovered quickly that there were at least two youth 'cultures'; those who lived in the day time, because they had jobs, and those whose waking hours began mid afternoon and extended until the early hours of the morning. A number avoided work, or left their employment, because their friends kept different hours and they were lonely and felt excluded from the action.

It was a fairly traditional Anglo-Catholic parish, with its own primary school, and a thriving social club in the crypt of the Church. My 'boss' had (and still has) a flair for liturgy and attention to the 'minute particulars of detail', which he believed was a way of showing care and love. It was a phrase he repeated *ad nauseam*, but he was right. He believed in a highly visible priesthood and we wore cassocks around the parish. He once banned me from a Church service when the bishop was due to be present, because I had taken both of my cassocks to the dry cleaners and had forgotten to collect them!

In an attempt to reach the myriads of young people who roamed around the local council estates, I took on the running of a disco for teenagers in an old church hall at one end of the parish. The boss had done the same when he was a curate. It was my attempt at evangelism, but if that most difficult yet central enterprise of the Church's life can be described as 'make a friend, be a friend, and then bring your friend to Christ', this work for the Lord was very much at the 'make a friend' stage of the process. Aside from the funeral of a dead teenager, and my farewell eucharist as curate, hardly a young person I encountered through the disco ever came to Church. Actually, I exaggerate. I remember a precious moment one Sunday when, during the first part of the liturgy, a teenager from the disco ambled in and took a seat in the back row. During the intercessions I closed my eyes in thanksgiving to God, that one of his little ones had at least crossed the threshold. By the time I opened my eyes, ready to greet him warmly at the sharing of the Peace, he had left!

Still, years later I am in touch with some of those youths, notably the ones who helped in the leadership of the disco, and I know that some have found their way into the Christian community, or arrived on a priest's doorstep when they were in trouble. They called me 'Linds' or 'Dad'. They still do.

Hundreds of teenagers, black and white, 'Walworth Roaders', 'Bermondsey Boys', girls and lads from Peckham and further afield, made their way to Surrey Square for the 'Brother to Brother' disco, named after two brothers who were the disc jockeys. A woman who ran a leather stall in East Street market ran the food bar with a rod of iron. I never enquired too closely as to why or how she managed to entice all the good-looking lads to join her behind the bar selling Mars bars, Coke, and some pretty revolting non-alcoholic beer. She was 'mouthy' and a local, which of course I was not. I used to sit on a stool at the door, trying to hide my fear of these teenagers, most of whom were twice my size, quick witted and dismissive or, at best, disinterested in me or the Church. But in order to be alongside them I hit on an idea. I went out and bought myself some designer jeans and a leather jacket. I drew the line at a fiendishly expensive 'Burbery mac', the designer status symbol of the time, worn by the kids in rain, hail or summer heat.

From 7.30 p.m. I would perch on the stool, trying to look cool, collect their 50 pence entry fee and check their membership cards. I even started chewing gum (they all did), and I listened hard to some of their phrases and terminology and started including it in my own vocabulary.

Barry Knight helped keep the tightly packed, hormonally charged hall under control. He was very big and very black, a surveyor of the scene, a leader of the pack. I understand he is even now a 'roady' for some big name pop stars. We got on well, and that helped. More than once he was my mouthpiece.

I'll never forget the night he called me over for a quiet word – almost impossible in the midst of the thump of the music and the general cacophony of voices. Once cosseted in the back room which acted as an office, I think I can remember the short but humiliating conversation, word for word.

'Hey, Father, what's that you're wearing?' 'Do you like it?' was my reply, chewing my gum, and pulling myself up to my full five-foot eight-and-a-half, against his six-foot plus, proudly displaying the leather jacket over my clerical collar, my hands in my jeans pockets. His response was devastating. 'Do you think, even in this light, that you look like a teenager? Why don't you go and put your dress on?' He meant my cassock of course. The lesson was clear. It's one I have never forgotten. Be yourself. Be yourself, even when you think being yourself might mean it takes longer to be accepted or listened to. Be yourself, because in the end people, especially young people, will discover when you're not. They hate humbug. These teenagers passed me in the street, wearing my cassock, and suddenly, in the half gloom of a dingy parish hall, I am pretending to be one of them in jeans and leather! My strategy and attempt to get alongside them in designer clothes was mistaken.

So I put my cassock back on, and stopped imitating the language of a south London teenager. It didn't suddenly mean that teenagers started to relate and talk with me, for the chasm between them and the Church was too great to be bridged in a couple of hours on a Wednesday night when the last thing on their minds was God!

Most didn't give a thought to the effort and energy, or the risk, I was taking even laying the disco on and many simply thought I was doing it to make money. But, over a period of time, some young people did make their way to my front door, fairly anonymously of course, to talk or seek advice. And I felt more relaxed!

Another lesson was learnt not long after, one which I have taken with me into every other place I have ministered and, in a strange way, was a good preparation for ministry as a bishop. Again Barry Knight was a prophet in the midst! A teenage lad, a 'Walworth Roader', had been murdered walking over Dunton Bridge, outside a fairly notorious pub, considered to be Bermondsey territory. London remains a mass of small villages. He was a boy who wore a lot of gold. His father, whose funeral I later took, was in prison, itself giving a certain caché to the boy. He was the sort of lad people wanted to know, and his own power lay in the decisions he made about whom he spoke to. In life, I never received more than a nod as he strutted down the Walworth Road. His death changed my relationship with the young people of the area.

Barry and the other leaders of the community decided to have a benefit night for the boy's mother in another local church hall. He called at my flat, asked me to come along and say a few words, adding 'And Father ... wear your dress.' Dressing up was an important part of youth culture in Walworth. As I have remarked, designer labels were important. The youths used to say that you could tell a social worker or probation officer from a mile away by the scruffy way in which they dressed. It brought derision. So I wore my 'dress'. When I arrived at the hall, it was pretty much out of control. A lot of underage children had poured a lot of beer and spirits down their throats (and seemed to have poured a lot more on the floor in the process). Boys were jumping up and down to the music chanting 'Walworth, Walworth, Walworth!' There were all the seeds for some really violent behaviour and reprisals, a matter I had already discussed with the local police. Aside from sliding on the slippery floor as I got on to the stage to speak, and a faulty microphone, I managed to get the attention of the assembled multitude.

In the midst of my talk, I told them it would be just as sad if a Bermondsey boy had been murdered, or a Bermondsey mother in mourning. There was deafening silence, then a hiss. Then they booed me out of the place. It was a lonely walk through the housing estates to my flat. But I learnt my second lesson, and it was about the loneliness of leadership, and a little of the cost of saying what you believe to be true. There was nothing especially heroic about it, and I was not in any danger, but I knew I was risking what little relationship I had with the local teenagers, but I had to say it.

The next day, Barry Knight rang on my doorbell, and shouted up to my second floor window, 'You were right Father, but you shouldn't have said it!'

This reminiscence may seem an exercise in middle-aged nostalgia, light years away from the ministry of a bishop as an apostle for youth, and certainly is, at least in terms of the localized and sustained ministry possible for a minister living in a fairly tightly knit community, and yet the two lessons about being myself, and the risk of unpopularity, even to the point of temporary alienation from the community I longed to connect with, inform my work with the teenagers of this diocese even now. And the effort of trying to reach children beyond primary school age who were not the children of Church-attending families, and therefore beyond the period of churchy interest acceptable in society at large, has been a pertinent reminder of the truth that to connect with young people involves travelling to the edge of the institution, taking only the bare essentials. It requires a willingness to move into unknown territory, beyond the polite society of the initiated who know one's 'position', and tend to tell the bishop what he wants to hear. And it involves a willingness to be educated, sometimes learning to understand a new language and way of seeing, and an acceptance that the person you love, Jesus, and the community you love, the Church, is so unwittingly overladen with its own culture that it risks failing to convey its message, however much it attempts or longs to do so.

In all three synoptic Gospels there comes a decisive, surely frightening moment when Jesus sends the disciples out in mission. In a rehearsal of their post-Pentecost vocation when, equipped as apostles with the gift of Holy Spirit, they were propelled out of the Upper Room into the insecurity of the open streets, Jesus empowers and sends the friends he has called to minister in his name. That the experience would not be easy and, indeed, at times prove demoralizing is presumably a reason why, in his divine wisdom, he sent them out two by two. Having called them initially because he wanted to be in company with them, a reassuring thought to which bishops as much as other ministers need to cling, he sends them to preach and to heal and reconcile. But Jesus makes it clear that they are to travel light. St. Mark's account allows the disciples to carry a staff, which at least gives their successors a crozier to hold on to, but otherwise, in all three accounts of the sending, it is as if the effectiveness of their ministry is somehow dependent on being stripped of those props which one might generally expect to be part of keeping body and soul together, so they become totally dependent on the truth and power and love of the One who sends them. In our context those props might include unnecessary bureaucracy, inappropriate expressions of hierarchy or dependence upon the security which comes from being part of the Establishment, the use of exclusive religious language, the authority we have to send others in our stead, or of hiding a little behind the business and busyness of Church life.

Of course, in the English parish scene, and my limited experience of other 'western' parts of the Communion suggests to me there are parallels; it has been the younger clergy who are expected to go to the edge, forging links with young people. My own testimony bears witness to this model. It often works, and many a thriving youth club is the result of endless hours of attention and love poured in by the young deacon or priest. In part this is because the curate is closer in age and outlook to the young people themselves. But I believe there is more to it than that, and it affects how bishops might approach a renewed enthusiasm and commitment to personal engagement with young people.

The curate is very much on the edge of the institutional Church. Newly ordained and without the responsibility of the rector or vicar, he or she is not so identified with the endless bureaucracy and administration that seem an inevitable part of Church life. Frustratingly, the less people actually come to Church, the more paper and brown envelopes there seem to be! Unlikely to be involved in committee life there is more time to be around, time to wait for opportunities and to have the trivial conversations often necessary before important issues emerge. Young people tend to be both immediate and laid back, so that events and situations rarely happen too long in advance. Set free from most of the managerial responsibility, and probably a full diary, the curate can often be the most apostolic and outward-going on the team, and may know more people on the fringes or outside the Church than his 'boss'.

All that is very good, but the curate is not enough! While it may be argued that he or she is a representative person, ministering in the name of the Church and with the bishop's licence, if young people are to be drawn into the life of the Christian community, the community and its leaders need to be involved in the drawing in, lest it appear that the curate or licensed youth workers are, as it were, working in spite of, or even in opposition to the institutional Church, or that work with young people, or the provision of an environment which listens and responds to young people, and allows them to contribute and speak, be limited to a phase in a priest's ministry, when he was blissfully free and energetic, and to which he looks back with nostalgia.

None of this emphasis on the ordained ministry is, of course, to deny the often heroic and brilliant work undertaken by parents and laymen and women in fostering the Christian faith of young people, and indeed it is true that the best evangelists of young people are other young people. Yet I would contend that unless the bishops are themselves seen to be reaching out to young people, engaging, listening to and teaching them, it is unlikely that the Church at large will seriously reorientate its priorities and finances towards a generation more connected with each other through mass media, advertising and the internet than ever before, and yet never less connected with the Body of Christ.

I recently came across these almost feisty words from a speech by an Anglican theologian, to an Anglo-Catholic congress in London in 1930.

> Taught by the New Testament, we are bound to think of the Episcopate as preserving the witness of the apostles and to demand this of the Bishops. The Bishops are not mystical persons to whom we owe some strange kind of undefined mysterious obedience. The Bishops are responsible to bear witness to Jesus Christ, the son of God, and to hold the Church to that witness.

Edwyn Hoskyns' affirmation of the bishop's ministry does not speak directly about witnessing among young people, so much the unconnected generation to the Church, but it must surely include them, and even if first spoken to Anglo-Catholics, his demand would surely find support from all traditions of Anglicanism. It's a call to seize hold of the gift which bishops received at their ordination. In his second letter to the young Timothy, Paul encourages him to 'stir up the gift you have received through the laying on of hands'. Indelible though Orders may be, they are not to be viewed as a gift possessed. Rather, they are as fire, a flame in need of fanning. Powerful, warming, alive, always the same and to be trusted, yet dynamic, spirited and constantly surprising. In the midst of all the administrative and managerial expectations which we lay upon our bishops, there is surely the need to reclaim the ancient title and vision of bishop as 'successor of the apostles'. I sense an embarrassment among those who have received this mandate to claim it, perhaps because we interpret this succeeding in monarchical and authoritarian terms, rather than as leaders supernaturally gifted in evangelism and mission. In claiming the title, so we bishops must claim the gifting, and in claiming the gifting must accept the work as a mandate from the Lord, a work and gift we pass on to those we ordain and confirm. And while the bishop has a care for all age groups in society and the Church in our own day, it is surely not amiss to suggest that there be more emphasis on apostolic work among young people!

Early in 1998 I was in Texas leading a couple of short parish missions. In one parish I spent Sunday afternoon with a fairly large group of teenagers. Relaxed and fun, they were dressed in a variety of ways as one would expect of any similar group. As I tried to speak to them about the resurrection of Jesus and what it may mean for their lifestyle, I noticed that just about all of those sitting on the front row were wearing a similar wrist band embossed with four letters, W.W.J.D. I was intrigued by this, and asked them what it meant, explaining that I had seen it etched on a wooden cross for sale in a Christian bookstore the previous weekend.

The young man who spoke up, looked at me with a look not unknown to anyone who deals with young people – a mixture of condescension and amused disdain! W.W.J.D.? The letters stand for 'What would Jesus do?' I admit my first reaction was to dismiss this as just another American gimmick, but the lad concerned gave me his wristband and I've worn it often, and certainly used it as a basis for sermons. I have found that it captures people's imagination, and not simply the young. Of course America is a peculiarly church-going nation, especially in the South, but it is a wonderful thought that, in the midst of all the pop, sports and media opinion formers, many young people, known because of their indefinability as 'Generation X', identify themselves with such an uncool question, and are willing to witness in this way. W.W.J.D. is a complex question of course, for it's surely difficult to know what the people I know and love best will do, or even to know what I would do myself in many situations. But these young people were attracted by the reliability of Jesus, his consistency, his outgoingness and his self-giving; that in him there was no two-mindedness at all. At a youth synod in my episcopal area, it was an hour-and-a-half spent in front of a crucifix, expressing in visual form the answer to that question, which provided a transforming moment for many of the participants. As I have talked around this question with young people, I have come to realize that in beginning with the person Jesus, I am led inevitably to the Bible and the Church.

This may tell us something about an appropriate evangelistic approach today, an approach which is something of a reversal from strategies of the past, when the Church provided many of the organizational belongings in society, and through attracting people to them, could then introduce them to the person, Jesus. Indeed up until a generation ago, people were joiners.

For reasons which are complex and go way beyond the remit of this chapter, we are now living in an anti-institutional culture, suspicious and cynical of organizations; it matters little whether it be government, monarchy or Church. Let me reflect further about this anti-institutionalism and the heightened emphasis on the individual, by thinking again about the wristband. It is surely true, that no young person, and perhaps one must admit not many adults, would wear a band with the letters W.D.C.S., 'What does the Church say?' Mention the Church and her teaching, begin a sermon with the words 'Holy Mother Church says . . .' and the eyes of young people simply glaze over. They are not interested. They simply assume it has nothing to do with them. They generally consider the gap between what little they know to be the ideals of Jesus and the way the Church lives too great – its divisions and manifest fallibility so evident that it simply doesn't warrant a hearing. This is painful to accept, and it is not necessarily true, but in evangelistic endeavour, if we are to be heard, we must begin with the preconceptions of those we seek to convert.

But mention the Scriptures and the person of Jesus and many are intrigued. Somehow the Scriptures seem less tainted and retain a purity. The Word and the words of Jesus are not associated with the failures of this present age, or the endless and empty chatter of a world full of throwaway lines and empty promises. A young university student I met recently in his College bar had nothing but suspicion for the Church, in part because he already knew that the demands of commitment and its moral standards would challenge his own present lifestyle, and yet he told me he considered Jesus to be the most fascinating 'philosopher' who ever lived. The temptation was to defend the Church, but the better approach was to talk about this 'philosopher', Jesus. And, of course, without labouring the point to him, to bring to our discussion the wisdom and insight of the Church and her reflections about the true identity of the man Jesus, who continues to tantalize and torment, and whose name, 2000 years later, is to be found around the wrists of the young.

So how is the bishop, in an intense way so much the embodiment of the institution, to minister with young people and bridge this gnawing gap, and so encourage others identified with the structures to do the same? Of course, he cannot collude with those who would seek to separate Jesus from the Church for he knows the theological nonsense of such a division, and, indeed, that his own position and authority to speak is dependent on a divine commission, to say nothing of his baptismal connection from which there is no escape! Desperately aware of the Church's failures as well as her heroism, he may not abandon her as he seeks to present Christ to the world and young people. Living with the wheat and the tares, and knowing that he is himself a mixed blessing, a bishop must demonstrate his love for the Church, a love which is not based on her faithfulness (for that is at times ambiguous), but because of his belief in the Church as a divine institution, an intended instrument and sign of the Kingdom. Like Newman, he must hold the Church in veneration 'for the love of Him alone'. He loves the Church because Jesus loves her.

However attractive it might be to jump on the anti-institutional bandwagon and collude with a disdain for the Church even in an effort to evangelize, a bishop may not. For he knows that Jesus and the Church are bound up with each other. It is his body, the extension as it were, of the Incarnation, and while Jesus will not be trapped in the Church, he can be found in her, and if his Spirit is not limited to the Church's own sphere of activity, nor God limited by his own sacraments, these are places in which he can be encountered most powerfully. Jesus, through his Spirit, makes humble procession when his Word is proclaimed and the Spirit hovers over the elements of bread and wine to make sacrament. As surely as he was present touching young people in his midst, so he touches now through these gifts. A bishop's own experience of Christ through these gifts is enough to encourage him to believe that they can also be a feeding ground for young people who are hungry like everybody else!

But the bishop must foster a paradox in his own life if he is to touch the hearts of young people. He must embody the institution, trust wholeheartedly to the gifts Christ has entrusted to his Church as places of divine encounter, indeed seek to make these attractive and attracting, and yet he must seek to sit lightly to it, using his authority to strip away unnecessary bureaucracy and travel to its margins. As he seeks to fulfil his calling as apostle, he should seek the grace to have about him that which is of Peter, as the rock on which the Church is built, entrusted with Christ's authority to forgive sins and proclaim the Gospel, and that which belongs to the apostle Paul, who was always pushing the boundaries, travelling to the edges to speak about Christ. There are plenty of people who 'know' he is the bishop, and will understand the protocol of how he is to be treated, and know his authority. Those involved in the institution will know how to play the game, if only to be secure in their own place within it. But he must take the risk of going in the midst of those who will not automatically assume that he has authority, or that he has something to say which is worth hearing, or who simply won't understand what a bishop is! He takes to those edges where young people are the very gifts they will not, because of the culture, generally bother to search out in our worshipping communities. And he must encourage and challenge the local Church, which remains the best hermeneutic of the Gospel, to explore ways of including young people in the celebration of worship, and in the formation of the common mind.

The primary pearl of great price the bishop, indeed any evangelist, takes to every personal encounter is the Word of God. Indeed, one might better say that the bishop is agent for the Word, who makes his way in humble procession towards young people as surely he did during his earthly ministry, and with as much love and longing. The Word made flesh approaches through his Spirit and a divine encounter results. This Word which approaches is God's revelation of himself, and it is in historic realities that the revelation takes place; to this man Abraham; to these people, the Jews; in this man, Jesus; to Paul on the Damascus Road; to these young people in this parish, or school or hanging around outside McDonald's! This is the way of the Incarnation, and the Church and the bishops must seek to present the Word in a way which makes a connection, or rather, be sure that the transitory elements of 'culture' in the Church do not hinder an encounter between the Lord of every culture and young people. With humility, prophecy, gentleness and judgement, and yet with a clear vision of his essential vocation, and of all that was needful, the Word made flesh mingled as a trans-forming presence with the culture he encountered. As I reflect upon my disco days, I was not conscious enough of the need to travel with the Word of God, or confident enough that the gifts he offers could break through or be presented in ways which might touch the lives of young people. I lacked the imagination.

The Word which approaches can be understood and experienced in a variety of ways, most known to Him alone. The Word as Christ can break through inspite of all, and seems frequently to do so, especially in person to person encounters. So I know, and I don't expect this is an untypical scenario, of a young person who was invited, not to join the 'organization', but to attend a one-off event, our diocesan youth camp, by a boy who was connected because his family attended a local Church. In the relaxed and slightly chaotic manner of the camp and in company with others of his own age and adults who cared about them, the 15-year-old experienced the Word as Scripture. This meeting happened through a certain amount of preaching and teaching by leaders, including the bishop who spent some time at the camp, not only in worship, but just 'chilling out' around the site. But the Word in Scripture came to meet this teenager as he sat outside the marquee with a number of other young people as they read and explored it, with all the freedom to misinterpret it and discover its truth for themselves.

Having been encouraged to worship at the local Church his friend attended, he began to feel at home, and discovered that mixing with people of all ages, including the elderly, was a joy he hadn't expected; that age need be no barrier, for the Holy Spirit is a youthful Spirit! He encountered the Word which approached him through the ministry of the bishop in the Sacrament of Confirmation, the bishop first having met with him and the other candidates to talk and seek to be a brother as well as the bishop. Perhaps with only a dim awareness, he met Christ in Holy Communion in a parish working hard to celebrate the liturgy with a mixture of mystery and informality, as befits those who worship one who cooks breakfast yet whom no one dares ask his name. Sometime later as he struggles to pray, the Word seems to call him to learn the guitar, though he has no musical training at all. Pick it up and play! This has led to a wonderful ministry of music in his local Church, and among the young people of West Sussex, and even to leading evening worship at the Lambeth Conference!

In all of this, generally from a distance, but at other times in a more intense way as his bishop, I have been involved. A few months after my episcopal ordination, I had been moved and challenged by a report of an encounter between a group of Australian journalists and some young people from Kracow in Poland. Faced with the appointment of the almost unknown Karol Wotjila as Pope, the journalists had heard that a sporting event had brought young people from his see city to Australia. There was nothing else to do but meet them in the vague hope that they might know something of him. When asked if they knew the new pontiff, the reply came 'Of course, he is our bishop.'

I have been surprised by how pleased young people are to see the bishop. I do not believe that it is entirely personal, though I hope that's part of it, and I certainly do not believe it is dependent on my being a comparatively young bishop. At 42, I am 'old' by their standards, however I do make a conscious effort to listen to youth music and culture, but am always happy to admit that I don't understand it, and can't keep pace with it! I don't stand on my dignity, nor pretend to be one of them. When speaking to young people I try hard not to use unnecessarily ecclesiastical language, and try to scratch where they itch. Many New Testament words figure in their music: world, flesh, truth, pain, now, the future, seeking, weak, strong, love, spirit, even God! I have also learnt to enjoy a more laid back approach to hierarchy and liturgy, though I am unafraid to wear my 'dress'! At a recent youth camp I celebrated and preached at the Eucharist. My episcopal throne was a blow up chair, which left me literally lurching from side to side; there was lots of singing and praising; the ministry of the Word included a homily, and then small groups all over the camp site with some questions from me to guide discussion. Then followed a sort of Saturday morning TV-style chat show for a while, with sofas and a compère with a variety of mad-cap, sort-of Gospel-centred activities, a couple of very laid back testimonies and competitions. The sharing of the Peace was expressive to say the least, after which came the Eucharistic Prayer. In spite of all it was comparatively easy to command silence and ask for respect for those who were to receive communion. It is possible to celebrate sacraments with young people. They know that words are not enough, and they enjoy action and symbols. And they have little or none of the churchmanship prejudices and allegiances of older Christians, and they can be alarmingly ecumenical! There was a mingling of the contemporary and transitory youth tradition or 'culture' expressive of the camp and its community, with the abiding Tradition, which we pray becomes as salt or leaven. It was alive. It's a very different scenario to the Sunday Communion in the local parishes of course, but there are lessons to be learnt. It was unafraid and trusting.

Of course, a particular event for young people led and encouraged by the bishop is one thing. Finding appropriate means by which young people who have found something of a home in the Church can contribute to decision making, to contemporary presentations of the Tradition in our liturgies, and in the setting of our priorities, is another.

To foster the engagement of the bishop with young people in the diocese of Chichester and to give them an authentic voice, we have created occasional youth synods. Far from being put off by the word 'synod', most had no idea at all that Anglicans meet in synods. Basing our life on Acts 2:42 and trusting to it as a dynamic which keeps the group faithful and focused on the Truth, it provides a relaxed opprtunity to rub shoulders, teach and listen to some 60 or so young people from a variety of parishes across the episcopal area.

The most recent synod, entitled 'Called to Account', took as a theme Peter's exhortation to be 'always ready to give a reason for the hope that is in you'. The participants met in small groups with questions to focus their thoughts, but they met without adult participation. Using the facilities and calling upon the hospitality of the local parish, the young people stayed in the homes of worshippers. The worship was a balance of Word, Sacrament and stillness. It was at this gathering that the prolonged time before the crucifix had such a profound, even converting effect.

So that the synods are not simply laid on, some young people are involved in the planning, and introduce the discussion sessions. I couldn't believe my luck at the first synod when a participant, in speaking about life-changing experiences, testified about his confirmation! The small groups which meet throughout the synod form resolutions – matters they want to put before the Church. I receive these quite formally, sitting silently in my 'throne', and then seek to respond, not only to thank them for their effort and wisdom, but also to challenge their prejudices and blinkeredness when necessary. The resolutions are sent to all the PCCs of the diocese, with a request that they reflect upon them, and a response to the bishop is requested. This has caused consternation to some PCCs, irritation in others, but many have responded to the challenges from the young people, and it has led to some action. I have no doubt that the fact that the synod is an episcopal initiative adds weight and heightens the impact. The next strategy is a series of meetings with children from secondary schools. It will take time, and it's a frightening thought!

None of this is earth shattering, and is a drop in the ocean when one considers the thousands of young people in Sussex who have not yet heard, or whose ears have been dulled to the Word. But it represents a genuine attempt to walk faithfully in the footsteps of the apostles, to claim the apostolic gift which Christ has entrusted to his bishops and to the whole Church, and to make use of that gift and to shift priorities, so that I may be known as an apostle for youth, and that even some might say, 'Of course! He is our bishop!'

# 7

# Jesus Christ
## The Lasting Legacy of Africa's Youth

*Emily Choge*

What is Africa bequeathing its youth? Many social and economic problems plague the continent as we enter the next millennium, so it is important to be clear about what we want for our young people. Many nations, and indeed all parents, are asking this question. Africa has come of age only recently, and therefore we have the opportunity to learn from the mistakes of the West. We're also lucky to have a rich heritage and strong traces of our traditional past, which unfortunately we're too ready to discard. In looking at the range of legacies, this chapter will show the strengths, and demonstrate the weaknesses, of what we're left with. We'll study the aspirations of our youth and how they fit with what their parents want for them. Then we'll look at the legacy of Jesus Christ, and how that has equipped us to stand at the crossroads of modernity and traditionalism.

## Education

Many African countries spend a large part of their budget on education. They made education a priority when they realized colonial powers had left them with few educational resources following independence. Ignorance, along with disease and poverty, was one of the major ills they resolved to overcome. Today in Kenya, schools have very high prestige value. Business people regard schools as a good investment.

What I call a craze for education has reached alarming proportions. Educational institutions, from kindergarten to university level, charge fees on a colossal scale. Only the wealthy can afford them. There are many boarding schools that charge extraordinarily high fees. To make matters worse, there is no pressure to account for how the funds are spent. Much of the money is not channelled into the education of the children. Instead it goes directly into the pockets of directors. Some headmasters in government schools are ready to misappropriate funds in order to build their own private schools.

Parents frustrated with the Kenyan system are often prepared to put their children into foreign schools in the country, mainly British and American. Then the parents are often willing to incur the expense of sending their children to universities abroad. Sometimes they are able to secure scholarships for their children, or raise funds through other means. Such parents are generally not concerned about their children's exposure to the values and culture of the other country. When they leave the country, many of their children have not even worked through the traumas associated with adolescence. Some never recover from the disorienting experience of education abroad.

There is an unrealistic expectation that education is the panacea for society's ills. Parents give their children an education as an investment for the future. They expect them to secure well-paid white-collar employment after they complete their education. Africa's high level of unemployment has had a particularly devastating effect on young people. One writer notes that each year almost 400,000 young people enter the job market in Kenya alone. Only one-quarter of these have a reasonable chance of employment. Even university graduates are not assured of jobs.

To make matters even worse, the Structural Adjustment Programmes imposed by the World Bank, the IMF and other donor agencies of the West has made the job market even more precarious. Governments are forced to retrench a large number of workers at an early age – in Kenya, a government decided to retire 60 per cent of the teachers in order to resuscitate the ailing economy. The effect of such measures is the frustration of parents' hopes for the education they can bequeath to their children.

Aside from the problematic job market, parents are now realizing that education does little to contribute towards their children's moral development. Education is geared to the attainment of certificates, not character. As a result there is a moral decline evident in the current generation of young people. In 1994 we witnessed the St Kizito incident in Kenya. After a number of students rampaged, several were killed and girls were raped and molested. This is not an isolated incident. Around three times a year, students have gone on strike in many schools. They have resorted to vandalism, destruction of property and other violent behaviour. They demonstrated their frustration when a power-cut interrupted their viewing of a 1998 World Cup football game by looting nearby shops.

There are also problems associated with the students' large workload. Because most parents have high expectations, their children are subject to an unreasonably high level of pressure. They are expected to complete a large amount of homework and extra tuition outside normal school hours. This keeps them up as late as midnight, and causes them to rise as early as 5 a.m. As a result, some develop psychological problems and drop out of school. Fortunately the Kenyan Government is now reviewing its demanding education system.

## Health

Aside from education, African parents want to provide for their children's good health. At the time of independence, the governments of Africa invariably noted the importance of health, and they allocated their resources accordingly. There has been a measure of success. The child mortality rate has been reduced, and the population is growing at an alarming proportion. However, more recent economic constraints have caused these improvements to slow markedly. In most African countries, health facilities are still very poor. Kenya has realized it cannot provide full medical cover for all its citizens. It has, consequently, introduced cost sharing. This has placed a heavy burden on low-income families. The problem is compounded by the practice of medical personnel misappropriating government medical supplies to use in their private medical clinics. Good health care, available in private clinics, is beyond the reach of most people in Africa because of the cost.

It should also be noted that a narrow definition of health prevails. There is little or no recognition of the value of holistic health. In traditional African society, there was an important social dimension to health care. This is consistent with the biblical understanding of wellbeing that is translated as 'Shalom'. It's no wonder, therefore, that Africa is facing many ills, including civil wars, ethnic violence, drug abuse and AIDS.

## Wealth

It is a well-known fact that African nations are among the poorest nations of the world. It is therefore understandable that governments and parents want to leave something for their children. They do this in the form of property, particularly land. Before colonialism, land was communally owned. Now it is owned individually, especially in Kenya. Recently the 'grab for land' has reached alarming proportions. Everybody has been appropriating for themselves property meant for public use. Ethnic clashes have also been motivated by this drive for land and tangible property. This lust after material wealth has also led parents to neglect those very children for whom they are struggling to get the wealth. In many family homes, children rarely see their parents, especially their father. Parents rise at dawn while the children are asleep. They return home late in the evening when the children have gone to bed. The children do not have anybody to discuss their problems with. The only person they relate with is the maid or 'house girl'. There have been several incidences of abuse and neglect by house girls, not to mention bad habits and poor upbringing. African parents must ask whether they're seeking to give their children wealth at the expense of their souls, and what they really want to give them. Teenagers seeking the answers to life's questions need the attention of their parents. It's no wonder that they become involved in shady activities.

## Return to traditional lifestyle

Most parents, disillusioned with modern life, have advocated a return to traditional values. Such parents may be highly educated. However, when it comes to the circumcision of children, they will take them to their home village to get the operation using the traditional methods. Those who administer these rituals are not really the traditional experts. Consequently the children can easily suffer infection. It has been found that such parents still advocate female circumcision, even though it has been discouraged for health reasons. They also want to give their daughters away in marriage early so that they can receive the dowry. It is legitimate that we should not throw away our culture. The result of neglect-ing our traditions is what has caused these problems with our children's lack of values. A Kiswahili proverb says: 'He who dis-cards his culture is a slave'. So we should preserve our rich cultural heritage. However, in the wake of modern technological changes we should choose very carefully what we want to preserve. It is not reasonable to keep outmoded harmful practices for the sake of preserving 'culture'. For example, the institution of adult initiation, marked by several rites and which signified an important part of the life of the individual in his community, should be preserved. The values of courage, sharing, communal living and service to the community, which were instilled to the young people during this period, are missing in our society. These values should be empha-sized. The mode of *transmission* of these values may be changed, but the core values can still be preserved. It is to be noted that tribal sentiments have also been fomented in the name of maintaining culture. This especially comes to a head when young people choose not to marry from within their own communities. This is resisted by parents because they cannot understand how to cope with such a situation. Even professing Christians have been known to disagree with their children when it comes to this issue.

Therefore, a blind advocating of a return to a traditional lifestyle is not feasible. As mentioned above, we should be selective in what we preserve, so that we do not get just to copy Western values, that are not even our own.

## Religious legacy

Even though they do not like to go to Church, most parents in Kenya feel that children should have some religious affiliation. They encourage them to attend youth activities, even if they them-selves are not interested in religion. However most of the young people get confused when their parents bring them to Church but do not attend themselves. While this exposes young people to the Gospel, it is not an attractive model.

## The legacy pursued by the youth

Having seen what parents prefer to give their children, we will now see the preferences of the youth themselves. We'll also see whether the aspirations and desires of both coincide.

## A FASHIONABLE LIFESTYLE

Due to the influence of the media and globalization, there is a universal youth culture in most of our cities today. What the youth are wearing in America can be seen in most of the African capitals. They are keeping up with these trends regardless of whether the parents can afford it. This interferes with their application to their studies in school and some adopt harmful and destructive habits in order to maintain a lifestyle compatible with that of their companions.

Along with this, there is the pursuit of pleasure. The teenage life coincides with the time of discovery of new horizons. Young people want to experience everything, especially that which gives them a 'high'. For some, this results in drug addiction, which in turn ruins their future. We therefore have a high level of drug abuse, sexual immorality, and generally a reckless attitude to life among young people that is disheartening to parents.

## ATTRACTION TO THE URBAN CENTRES

Because the youth realize that they can only get a job in the modern urban centres, there is mass migration into these towns. They also feel the pull of the bright lights of the city. One author notes:

> The youth are not attracted by the style of rural life ... Because of these constraints many of the youth migrate to urban centres to look for the hoped for better economic options. Now while the youth exodus towards urban centres increases, the job opportunities there get less and less. This creates a very difficult situation for our youth and the undesirable outcome of it may be increased attitude of apathy, fatalism and delinquency among the youth of both sexes. Idleness induces some of the young people to indulge in sexual immorality, notwithstanding the problem of premarital pregnancies, single parenthood and the deadly disease AIDS which inevitably spreads faster in such circles. (AFER 1989: 214)

This shows that whilst urban life may promise much to the youth, it does not offer a lasting legacy for many of them. The same author notes that knowing that more than 85% of our people live in rural areas and about 98% of the national product comes from those areas what can we do to make them attractive to our youth? (AFER 1989:214).

CULTURE OF VIOLENCE

In order to release some of the tensions and frustrations of the modern lifestyle, youth have resorted to violent activities. Such tensions were diffused in traditional communities by giving the youth very useful and strenuous leisure, as well as creative activities, such as hunting. In the modern towns where leisure pursuits have been reduced to inactive video and TV, it is no wonder that we see such gross manifestations of violent activities. Leisure has also acquired a monetary value and so those who cannot afford the expensive sports resort to the crude methods. Most of the young people now in Africa have learned that in order to get things done one has to resort to violence. This has been noted in most of our schools, especially through the prevalence of various strikes, and yet this does not solve the problem but in fact it creates many more, and it is the youth and their parents who suffer because they have to incur costs.

## *Jesus Christ – the only lasting legacy for Africa's youth*

It is important to note that while the legacy of wealth, education, health, culture and religion may be attractive options for us to bequeath to our youth, we have also seen the short comings. It is when these things are presented as an end in themselves and as the ultimate goal in life that we present a lie, because they challenge the words of him who said 'I am the way, the truth and the life.' While secularization has taken its toll in the West, we still have the option in Africa to present the way of truth. Recent research showed that most university students who took religion as a subject did so on grounds of faith. So it seems that there is still hope for Africa' s youth to live for Christ. I believe that Jesus Christ is the hope for Africa because of these reasons.

1.   The rich religious heritage of Africa's past. Africans have been described as notoriously religious. All the dimensions of life had a religious component. All the African communities had a

concept of God as a supreme being. It is no wonder that Africans had no words for pagan or infidel, and belief in God was not in dispute. Africans viewed health in a holistic manner. They valued the ideals of solidarity, sacredness of life and the dignity of all people, especially the elderly. This is the rich heritage in which the Gospel of Jesus Christ finds fulfillment.

2. The Christian legacy of Africa. It has been observed that the Church in Africa has experienced phenomenal growth. Throughout most of East Africa, Christianity is the predominant religion. One author has observed that because the majority of the population in Africa is young, the African Church is young. This means that the composition of the African Church is young compared to that of Western countries, where it is difficult to find young people in Churches. Church is a very attractive option for the young people in Africa, who are generally gregarious, and like to gravitate towards their contemporaries. This is an opportunity the Church in Africa cannot afford to lose. They need to present the claims of Jesus Christ. Christ was himself a young person, who had a definite purpose and mission. If we do not present Jesus' claims in a credible manner, young people will be attracted to other religious personages who are common in Africa.

3. Personal heritage. Jesus Christ offers a meaningful personal relationship, which young people are looking for. This is not based on status, race or creed. They are accepted as they are, with no impositions. This is very attractive to the young person, who is seeking acceptance and a sense of belonging. Young people realize they have a friend in whom they can confide, even if the world does not accept them.

4. Communal heritage. Belonging to Jesus Christ has the added dimension of belonging in a family of believers. In this group, young people, especially those in the cities who have lost the support and security of the family home, will find others who can empathize with them. This communal aspect of the Church should be strengthened, so that the young people can find a place to interact, not only with those of their own age group, but also with older people, who are able to provide guidance.

5.  The mission heritage. The young person who comes to Christ
    finds that he not only gets a personal friend and a family. He
    also becomes involved in a task that has universal significance.
    Young people have very high ideals, and they have a sense of
    wanting to contribute to something. When they are not given
    this challenge and opportunity in the Church, then they look
    for it elsewhere. The popular adage that says that the youth
    are the Church of tomorrow has to cease, so that they can be
    acknowledged as the Church of today. In challenging the
    youth regarding this mission, Pope John Paul II, in his message
    to young people on the Fourth World Youth Day, had the
    following to say.

The world today is one great mission land, even in countries
of long standing Christian tradition. Everywhere today neo-
paganism and the process of secularisation present a great
challenge to the message of the Gospel. But at the same time
there are openings in our day for the proclamation of the
Good News. We see, for example a growing nostalgia for the
sacred, for genuine values, for prayer. And so today's world
needs many apostles especially apostles who are young and
courageous. You, young people have in a special way the task
of witnessing to the Gospel, the commitment to bring the
Gospel of Christ – the Way, the Truth and the Life – into the
third millennium, to build a new civilisation of love, Justice
and peace.

## Case studies

Last year I had the opportunity to attend a mission conference
organised by FOCUS (Fellowship of Christian Union Students), the
Kenyan branch of the International Fellowship of Evangelical
Students (IFES). It was attended by over 1000 young people from
the universities and colleges of Eastern Africa. The theme of the
conference was 'Who can but speak?' (Amos 3:8). The introduc-
tory remarks of the conference director, Calisto Odede, show that
youth are on target in trying to get a lasting legacy for Africa. He
noted

Africa seems to have very unique problems of its own. We live
in an environment that seems to growing less and less friendly

> to our survival. We are threatened by both the natural and political calamities. Included in the list are: wars, genocide, coups and countercoups, ethnic violence, corruption, famine, poverty and floods. Faced with all these circumstances including the inaccessibility of parts of our countries is possible for us to surrender even before we begin. Yet what Africa is looking for is a Prophet. Someone who seems to know where we are going or where we ought to go and can speak to our nations with a prophetic voice (Commission '97 Focus Booklet: 1).

These young people were serious about what they wanted, as they listened to messages about the context in which they are to exercise their prophetic task. These key messages focused on the various mission fields, such as the concrete jungle, the broken world, the Muslim neighbour, and speaking together in partnership in mission. In the workshops, the young people were exposed more to this mission as they learned about the importance of developing a Christian character and maintaining a witness though holy living – especially in their sexuality – through the seminar, Passion and purity'. The popularity of this seminar showed clearly that the youth desired to serve God with their sexuality. They also got guidance on being Christians in various professions such as in politics, business, in academia, and even how they should handle the sensitive issue of unemployment. The enthusiasm and serious-ness that these youth displayed showed that with such young people who have a zeal for Jesus Christ Africa will not be the same. Such conferences have gone a long way in influencing the direction of life for these students. Some have gone to the mission field. I know one who, as a result of Commission '88, started his mission organization and he is now reaching the communities in the Eastern part of Kenya who have been un-reached for a long time. This just goes to show Africa for Jesus Christ.

*A personal testimony*

I was born in a Christian home. From the time I was young I knew the claims of Jesus Christ because my parents took the trouble to teach me the Bible. I enjoyed reading the Bible stories because they were very real to me. My parents were not rich people and the only legacy that I have from them is walking with God. Like the Psalmist I can say, 'The boundary lines have fallen to me in pleasant places, surely I have a delightful inheritance'. But even as my parents gave me the legacy of the Gospel, they did not ignore my academic work. In those days many girls were not encouraged to go to school and, to make matters worse, I was born with a physical disability which further complicated things. But this did not discourage my parents from sending me to school. They took me to boarding school so that I would have the ease of going to school without being hindered by my disability. Being in boarding school enhanced my relationship to God because I realized that, without my parents nearby, I had no one else to turn to except God.

I then went to a former mission high school and I was involved with many Christian activities, but I knew in my heart that I had not chosen the way of Christ fully. When I was in the fourth form I went to a Christian rally. There I was challenged not just to remain in the crowd but to choose to follow Christ. The preacher challenged that us that day that Jesus had one bride and, like in a wedding, several of us escort the bride but we will not get to heaven. This challenged me to realize my position in Christ – that it did not depend on the faith of my parents, but that I had a responsibility to make my own decision. Since then my life has been a pilgrimage of learning and enjoying the friendship and intimacy of the Lord Jesus.

In campus life my faith faced a new dimension in that I was challenged to live my faith even in the face of opposition. I chose to do study to be a teacher with the option of teaching history and religion. In these two departments those who had a personal faith in Jesus Christ were ridiculed and thought to be silly. The thing that helped me to remain strong in my faith is that I looked at the lives of the lecturers: they did not portray a good example, so I saw that they did not offer a better alternative to the way I had chosen. I also had a group of friends to whom we gave peer accountability and this helped to boost my walk with God. I also met a Christian group whose main focus was to help young people to mature in their walk with God. They were interested in me personally and I felt that I mattered.

In my working life I have continued to appropriate the grace of God and meet him anew every day. I have also endeavoured to help young people to find this legacy of Christ, which I found when I was young and have not found him to grow stale. I have done this as I have ministered as a school teacher, as youth director in the Church while doing my graduate studies, and even as a lecturer in the university. I have attempted to show students that apart from excelling in academic studies, it is actually necessary have their priorities right, even as we seek first the kingdom of God.

## Recommendations

It is clear that in the midst of the transition Africa is now undergoing, the legacies that we want to leave our children have changed. We have noted that what we most value – education, health and wealth – will ultimately be destructive if they lack a spiritual component. In Africa we have not yet seen the full effects of embracing technological advances uncritically, but we can learn from the West. We do not have to wait for young people to turn to pagan and occult practices in order to fill the gap that has been left by the lack of emphasis on the spiritual values of a personal relationship with Jesus Christ. We have seen that the young are looking for satisfaction in pleasure and riotous living. However some have found the direction, and are making a lasting impact in their communities, because they dared to take the message of Jesus very seriously. In view of the above observations I recommend the following.

1.  A viable youth programme that is suitable to the context. The context we have now is a dynamic one and, as has been noted, the influence from the West is being embraced fast. We need to assess what we have in our hands as African people, especially with regard to the preparation of young people to be useful members of society. The traditional rites of passage – especially those that initiated the young into adulthood – can be adapted to the changing environment. In the Church tradition we have the rites of baptism and confirmation. These could be made more meaningful by coinciding these with the rites of initiation into adulthood. I know a rural Church that have modified the traditional entry into adulthood by introducing a Christian component to it. They circumcise boys communally (using modern methods so that a doctor is present). But they still observe the seclusion period. So boys stay away from

home and are taught the art of communal living. Additionally, they are taught their role and responsibilities in the Christian community which they now belong to. At the end of the session, which is about four or five weeks, they are welcomed into the community with much joy. The ceremony begins in the Church building, showing that these children are dedicated to God first, and the celebrations continue in the village.

2. The need to be committed to the young so that we can empathize with them as they go through this period of transition in their own living, as well as going through the traumas of the transition of society. There is a need to give more than lip service. It is important to realize that this part of the Church needs a permanent youth worker who can follow up their development. In one of the Churches I was ministering to in Nairobi, the Curate who was in charge of youth activities was transferred after every six months or a year. Therefore the young had to begin all over again in their new programmes. These was very discouraging to the youth and it was no wonder that this Church was losing members to other Churches that had well-developed programmes.

3. The need for new methods for ministering to the young. Most of the old teachers are used to the lecture method and just telling people, not expecting them to contribute meaningfully. Even in traditional African society where respect for adults was emphasized the youth were given meaningful tasks, so that they could have a sense of accomplishment. There is a need for interactive learning methods. As we noted above, the youth love to imitate and they also love music, so they can be involved in asking to skit the Scripture lesson or put it into a dance. In the youth group I ministered to I learned that, whenever there was a dance to be performed, the youth were involved with great enthusiasm. In relation to this the youth workers need to be trained and to be the kind of people that are ready to learn from the young.

4. The need for mentors. Young people are looking for role models to whom they can trust their lives. They look for those who are accomplished in various fields so that they can be encouraged that they can make it too. They need to see that the claims of Jesus Christ can actually be lived out in a practical manner by real people. They need adults who will

walk alongside them to help them along the way, who will not harass, embarrass nor threaten them. They need to be accepted as they are. I think we put too much responsibility on the youth worker. I suggest that the whole adult community of the Church needs to be educated so that they can support the youth workers as they try to guide the young ones into responsible membership of society.

5. The need to develop Family Recreation Centres. We noted above that there is a general trend of rural migration to the cities. In the village churches, where there are no facilities for recreation, these churches can get together and pool their resources so that they can provide these needed facilities. They can also identify places that young people and their parents can go for retreats at minimal cost. These may be waterfalls, springs, mountains etc. Sometimes we have isolated the youth so much that they tend to feel that they are a strange species. But I feel that if they are incorporated into the activities of the family and the Church with the rest of the members, they tend to develop into more balanced people. I remember one occasion when we had a Sunday School day at Church and the youth participated with the adults in making the day an exciting day for the children.

6. The need to challenge the youth to take the claims of Jesus Christ seriously, since he is the only one who can help to navigate the confusion of life. The words of Pope John Paul II come in handy again.

Have you discovered Christ who is the Way? Yes, Jesus is a way that leads to the Father, the only Way. Whoever wants to reach salvation must set out along this way. You young people very often find yourselves at cross-roads, not knowing which path to choose, which way to go, there are so many wrong paths, so many facile proposals, so many ambiguities. In moments like those do not forget that Christ, with his Gospel, his example, his commandments, and alone is the safest way, the way which leads to full and lasting happiness. Have you discovered Christ who is the Truth? Truth is the deepest need of the human spirit. Young people especially are hungry for the Truth about God and man, about life and the world. Have you discovered Christ who is the Life? Each of you is anxious to live life in its fullness. You live with great hopes, with so many plans for the future. But, do not forget that the true fullness of life is to be found only in Christ, who died and rose again for us (AFER 1989: 56).

*Conclusion*

We have seen that Africa is at the crossroads, caught between the values of the West and those of the traditional heritage. But in between there is also the alternative of Jesus Christ. I believe that as we take the claims of Jesus Christ seriously and apply them to our context, without blindly copying past customs, then we will survive the future able to look forward.

FURTHER READING

AFER, 31 no 4:1989
AFER, 38 no 1:1996
Djoeandy, Omar, *Perspectives on Leadership Training*, edited by V.B. Cole, R.F. Gaskin and R.J. Sim. NEGST, 1993.
Getui, M.N. 'Religious Aspects of Secondary School Life and their Effects on Youth in Kenya', unpublished PhD thesis, 1993.
Nasimiyu-wasike and D.W. Waruta (eds) *Mission In African Christianity: Essays in African Christianity*, Uzima Press: Nairobi, 1993.
Rice, Wayne, *Junior High School Ministry*, Zondervan Michigan Publishing House, Grand Rapids, 1987.

# 8

# Aussie Salvation:
## A Vision for Anglican Youth

## *Thomas Smith*

'Aussie Salvation: A vision For Anglican Youth', is an intriguing title to give an Anglican from Sydney to write. My overseas Anglican brothers and sisters tell me that Sydney Anglicans are known to be 'hard men' and to be somewhat 'in your face'. I don't know how appropriate that reputation may be, but I am convinced that the Anglican Church in Australia, and certainly in much of the West, has some fundamental 'hard' thinking to do about the place of young people within it.

This chapter will explore the current dilemma of identity forma-tion that has developed for individual young people, communities and nations. The old intuitive understandings of identity formation no longer work due to the profound changes that are occurring in the micro and macro contexts in which individuals and communi-ties seek meaning and satisfaction. The Youth Ministry notion I am propounding is that the Church can best help young people by talking with them to develop an overarching Identity, which is formed by seeking to meet the expectations of Jesus Christ. In this way their expectations, values, attitudes and character become Christ-like.

But first I return to the phrase, 'A Vision For Anglican Youth'. This is an apt phrase to refer to the condition of the Anglican Church at the turn of the millennium. One obvious meaning of 'A Vision For Anglican Youth' concerns finding a vision for ministry to youth by the Anglican Church. I think that it is unnecessary for me to have to argue that the Western Anglican Church needs much more than an 'Anglican Youth Programme' or 'An Anglican Youth

Ministry Plan'. The statistics on Anglican Church youth attendance speak eloquently of the crisis facing our Church. We are in urgent need of a paradigm shift, that will give our Churches a vision and commitment for effective Ministry to Youth.

The second sense of 'A Vision For Anglican Youth' is equally vital to the future of the Anglican Church. It opens up the whole area of envisioning today's Anglican youth to develop *their* vision for taking the Gospel into their world. I think it is a mistake to ignore the great promise given by the Spirit-filled St Peter at Pentecost:

> And in the last days it shall be, God declares,
> I will pour out my Spirit on all flesh,
> and your sons and daughters shall prophesy,
> and your young men shall see visions.
> (Acts 2: 17)

That prophecy is to be fulfilled in our day too. We need, I believe, to raise adolescents who have the vision and courage to reach their generation and future youth generations with the Gospel. I intend to explore both senses of the phrase 'A Vision For Anglican Youth.'

### My Dream For Youth Ministry in the Anglican Church

I can dream, in the spirit of the Pentecost prophecy, of an Anglican Church which has an abundance of youth, many of whom seek to help others live as the Body of Christ in their national culture.

Therefore one outcome of this chapter is to identify some key principles for helping our Anglican youth become people who will speak God's word with power, because they have God's vision by which to challenge the Church and the world.

I believe that we must resist the temptation to accept quick and inadequate analyses of what is needed. The solution is definitely not the provision of more money and resources alone. Something much more fundamental is needed. It is ironic that within the history of the Church we have never known so much about youth ministry, and the rationale for doing it, whilst, at the same time, we have never faced such a crisis in ministry to youth and by youth.

I don't need to point out the parlous state of Ministry to Youth in the Western Anglican Church. Surveys such as that by the

National Church Life Survey, in Australia, and similar work in other countries, has done this adequately.

## The Need For a Paradigm Shift in Anglican Youth Ministry

Our Anglican Church is facing enormous changes as part of the greater international changes that are affecting every aspect of every individual's life. Just as our Western culture has undergone a paradigm shift from Modernism to Postmodernism, especially in many youth cultures, so the Anglican Church needs to go through a paradigm shift in the way it helps people develop a Christ-like Identity.

For me the critical challenge we Anglicans face is whether we will change our denomination's culture to provide a context where young people (and other sub-groups), can experience a worship culture that affirms their learning style and challenges them to want to have a Christ-like Identity. However, I fear instead we may remain a denomination that invites young people to join our current worship culture with its learning styles that were helpful to us when we were young, in the 1940s and 1950s.

## The Danger of Returning to the Glory Days of Our Youth

I need to identify the 'context' where we older Anglicans may be tempted to find security as we consider the processes involved in changing our ministry to youth. If we don't recognize this danger, it will catch us unawares and weaken our resolve to produce the best ministry to young people we can.

For those of sufficient age, there will be memories of the 'glorious days' of the 1940s and 1950s, when we had big youth groups in the western part of the Anglican communion. They were the days when many of today's Church leaders became Christians, through Christian Camping and vital university club work. They were also the days when many young Christians learnt to think rigorously, thanks to the work of C. S. Lewis.

Adolescent identity formation, in those 'glory' days was less fraught with the complexity of powerfully competing ideologies that exists today. Being an adolescent seemed easier then; gender roles were accepted by most people as definite and clear cut, sexuality was seen as a given, except for the 'unfortunate minority', and young people seemed free of the anxiety that adolescents felt in the 1980s and 1990s. A young person in the Church seemed able to form an identity, and to become a 'good' Anglican, without needing to think about it too much.

However, life is much more complex for adolescent development today. Now, young people are confronted by a plethora of identities within their multicultural societies. It is not just a matter of choosing which strata of society with which to identify, and perhaps which race and political elite. They now have to choose from a diversity of options for gender roles and sexuality. In nearly every culture where Anglicans are found, there is a superfluity of belief systems, each with its own inherent values and understandings. A young person is likely to learn about relationships from teenage soaps; to see in the media, politicians demean their opponents; and will have talked to peers who use friends' star signs by which to understand them.

We must face the reality that we cannot go back and try to use the youth strategies of our youth with today's youth. Today's young people are doing it tough, and would wonder at the naivety of the youth groups of our generation. This young generation is one of the most discerning generations ever seen. They will not accept our hope and meaning for life easily. They have been burned many times in their short, intense lifes. Family breakdown, high youth unemployment, and an apparent self-serving establishment have made them cynical of the generation of which the Church is seen to be a part. I think we have to 'do the hard yards' of youth dialogue if we are to be able to act and speak the Gospel within the culture of these young people we seek to reach!

### Identity – One Key to Effective Christian Youth Ministry

Not all is doom and gloom, however, for those seeking how best to minister to youth. We do have a natural point of connection with today's adolescents, namely an adolescent's identity development. Adolescence is the time when a person forms her incipient adult identity. For many of today's adolescents the development of their identity is one of their most difficult tasks. Our point of connection is our mission to help young people develop a mature adult identity.

An adolescent naturally develops her identity to enable her to relate, in a meaningful way, to others in every context of her life. Conversely, she also wants to relate to herself and to know herself in a meaningful way. Each adolescent is in the vital business of developing specific identities to enable her to fit into each of her social contexts, that is, to be able to operate so as to meet her own expectations as well as the expectations of others in each particular context. That way she will receive approval and acceptance based on her behaviour, instead of rejection and an experience of social failure.

For our part, we are eager to help the young person have the identity to which their Creator would lead them. This identity nexus between an adolescent's self-hood development and the church's mission is a unique opportunity open to us. I am therefore advocating that ministry focused on adolescent identity development be the paradigm shift for the Anglican Church's Ministry to Youth. This model provides a point of significant connection with young people and helps them meet their deepest needs, which are Spiritual.

But first let me define 'identity'. Identity can be a slippery word, sometimes meaning self, at other times a role someone is playing, or its meaning may even refer to a person's self-concept. Identity, as I use the notion, is the understanding a person has of herself, of how she will act in a situation where people have expectations of her that are different to the expectations she has for herself. Identity develops from the gradual integration of the values and self-expectations of her multitude of specific context identities. This core of values, expectations and integrated personal history, gives her a sense of continuity she will experience as her Identity, that is, her 'I am . . .'.

Research demonstrates that the context-specific identity a person develops arises from the way she perceives she must act in a particular situation (Askham, 1969 and Kondo, 1990). Each time the adolescent is in that particular situation she will have the same expectations of what others want from her and what she expects of the situation. Eventually she will develop a competence to act in accordance with those expectations of that context, and will, in effect, have developed an identity appropriate to it.

Indeed every adolescent in our society perceives themselves and others to have a wide variety of identities, because people act in a multitude of contexts (Askham, 1969 and Kondo, 1990). An adolescent will have an identity for each context she regularly experiences. For example, a schoolgirl will have one distinct identity in her maths class, whilst having a quite different identity on the netball court. Although it is, in effect, the same girl in each context, it is likely that she will have different goals, values and ways of expressing herself in each context.

Consider how an identity may develop in a girl who is new to a selective Anglican school. When she first comes to her school House she will not know the House norms, goals and ways of doing things. Typically, she will be quiet and will observe all that is happening. A teacher will address her, she will be introduced to the House, another girl will help her fill in her timetable. After a few days she will risk joining the conversation of those around her. If she acts in a way that accords with the House's expectations of an Anglican selective schoolgirl, then she will receive recognition and acceptance. If, however, she 'talks big' about her former school, she will soon find rejection and loneliness – and this is terrible because she is stuck with this group. Because she wants 'meaning in her House experience' she will develop a repertoire of expectations, values and a world view (i.e. an identity) that makes her a valued member of the House, according to her ability and personality (Kondo, 1990). Later, the girl's parents may hear friends say 'Look how she has developed an X House identity.'

A person's Identity contrasts with her contexts' identities. Her Identity could be thought of as her overarching Identity that forms, by choice, from across her contexts' identities. A clearly defined Identity enables the young person to have a set of integrated expectations, a repertoire of interpersonal skills and personal goals that provide direction for various types of social behaviour. It gives the adolescent a conception from which to behave in each social situation. Also, in cases in which the individual has a choice of action, a sense of Identity may aid her in deciding between a variety of different goals or motives for action (Ashkam, 1984).

Identity may largely be a social construct, to quote Kondo. Whether this is so or not, Identity is crafted by the many choices the adolescent has made in the many contexts of her life. For example, her family, school peer group, social peer group and sporting team. Christians have various contexts to offer to the adolescent for her Identity development too. There is the transcendent world of the Spirit, within the context of a loving community of prayer and service to God and His mission. The personal expectation of being an active member of the Kingdom of God in a hurting world will have a natural point of contact with the idealistic, justice-aware young people who make up today's youth.

## A Psychological View of the Factors of Identity

For those who may be interested in the dynamic factors of which Identity consists, I have deduced the following six:

- intentionality: the ability to be aware of oneself as a person who causes things to happen, because of one's personal goals and values
- confidence: a conscious trust in one's abilities arising from many successful experiences in various contexts and the belief in a 'natural' order in every context
- Values, goals and spiritual beliefs: the following of spiritual values, e.g., forgiveness
- Power: the ability to make things happen. For Identity, the 'service' use of power is highly valued
- Integration: a measure of the degree to which a young person has integrated her values, goals and expectations from their various contexts
- Mimesis: a person's choice to take their expectations from significant others; and to want to own the expectations of their perceived Transcendent Being.

## The Scriptures and the Development of Human Identity

I want to show how the notion of identity opens a 20th-century connection to vital New Testament concerns for the formation of a human's maturity. Note that when a person enters the kingdom of God, the greatest change he notices is not a sinless nature, nor instant righteous motivations. What is different for a new Christian is his identity as a child of God, with the desire to meet His expectations.

The Scriptures have much to say about the process of becoming a mature person of faith. Consider how the faithful Christian who regularly says the words of the Lord's prayer with meaning and faith, will find her identity become more Christ-like over time. This will occur because her expectations will be transformed as she says the Lord's prayer with meaning. She will perceive she need not be insecure about her life because God is in control ('who art in heaven'); she will want God to be honoured above all else, thus releasing her from her egoism ('Hallowed be thy name'); and she will develop values and goals based on the Kingdom of God – indeed she will transcend her own contexts by wanting the eternal context of His kingdom ('Thy kingdom come, Thy will be done on earth as in heaven').

And so on with the rest of the Lord's prayer. The person who prays the Lord's prayer in faith will have an Identity of deep confidence, from the knowledge that God will meet her physical needs, and she will become a forgiving person through the process of saying 'as we forgive those who sin against us'. That is how she will see herself!

### Giving Adolescents the Vision to Want to Meet God's Expectations

Adolescents respond enthusiastically to genuine encouragement, especially from older people. Christian leaders who give abundant encouragement and provide high expectations tend to form Christ-likeness in their youth group members. When these leaders also give Christian vision for their members' lives, the group members gain energy, direction and resilience, especially for when their Christian witness gets tough.

God's vision for His people, that they be His children, has a motivating effect we should not overlook. For example, Jesus' words, recorded in John 14:23, 'If a person loves me, he will keep my word, and my Father will love him, **and we will come to him and make our home with him**', produce a powerful resonance that transforms an adolescent's Identity. Her expectation's will be Godward, inward and towards other people. That is the effect of a relationship with God in Christ.

We proved the power of this Christian hope to motivate young people in parishes with little or no youth ministry. Young people who were discipled within the context of 'being a child of God', and 'wanting what God wants', often became involved in youth ministry in their own Churches as well as providing ministry in other Churches.

*Disciples' Groups Developed to Produce Christian Identity*

It was with the notion of Christ-like character formation in mind that a group of us developed a daring project in Sydney. In 1993, a group of people, committed to youth ministry, worked with me to develop a vision for fostering the development of a Christ-like character in young people, both inside and outside our Anglican Churches in the diocese of Sydney. Because we knew that identity was a social process, we made it a basic requirement that discipling would be a group process, with leaders whose lives would model Christ-likeness and provide Christ-like expectations of group members. We decided on two strategies to be used in the disciples' groups.

The first strategy was the verbatim sharing time. Each member would come to the meeting with an incident that occurred at university, work or school from the previous week. The incident would be an interaction where she may have been pressured to act according to a different set of values to her Christian ones. The purpose for the members of the disciples' group (they were in fact called disciples' groups), was to help the person become aware of significant personal values that may have been triggered by the challenge of the incident. For example, Sally shared about the confrontation she had had at College with another student, over who should sit in a particular chair! In response to gentle questions from other members of her disciples' group she said, ' Well I always sit in it and I didn't want to give into such an awful person.' Eventually she was able to scrutinize her unchristian value of 'only serve people who are worthy of your service'. She then reaffirmed her desire to meet Jesus' expectations and over the next week apologised to the other girl.

The second strategy was the 'goal/expectation' approach to Bible study (Smith, 1993). Members of the disciples' groups were encouraged to consider a Bible passage from the perspective of 'God is addressing our goals and values'. For example, in considering Jesus' teaching on 'The Vine and the Branches', (John 15: 1–11), the members would consider the following questions: 'What might you have to change in your life if you were to want your relationship with Jesus to be intimate?' 'How committed are you to living by Jesus' teaching; and what will this commitment cost you?'

Questions of this nature invited the youth group members to test their goals and values against the values and expectations expressed in the Scriptures. 'After all', the young people were challenged, 'don't people follow Jesus so that they can learn to see life as he sees it and to have his attitudes of service and love?' The response in terms of changed lives exceeded our hopes. For example, one young tradesman developed the trust to ask for support in overcoming his compulsion to hire erotic videos each month. His disciples' group met the challenge and supported him through his time of healing.

Our team took seriously the need to motivate the young people. They were invited to take personal goals that were the goals God offered. For example, they were challenged by that fantastic promise in St John's Gospel (chapter 1, verse 12); '**to all who received Jesus, who believed in his name, He gave the power to become children of God**'. The young people were encouraged to contemplate this promise, and to search their hearts as to whether there could be anything in this Universe that could be as wonderful for them as the fulfilment of this promise. They were able, by faith more than by experience, to conceive that what God want's for His people is so much better than anything they could imagine for themself.

The change in group identity, and personal Identity of the members, varied. However, the experience of the group the young tradesman belonged to is typica!. They provided two youth ministry weekend events for a country parish that was unable to provide any youth ministry for the young people in its area.

After the programme had run for 18 months we, at the Anglican Youth Department (now Anglican Youth and Education), researched the disciples' group project. The research instrument was crude – it sought to measure Christian commitment of the young people in youth groups. A scale of 1 to 5 for the increasing degrees of commitment was devised. The research was carried out across youth groups in the diocese to allow a comparison with other parishes. The criteria of the Level of Commitment Instrument are shown in the table opposite.

| Level of Commitment | Criteria ror Measuring Members' Commitment |
|---|---|
| 5 | Committed to Christ-likeness and involvement in His ministry to the world. |
| 4 | Committed to living a Christian life, having regular quiet times. |
| 3 | Committed to the group, God and Christian things, but may live differently with non-Christians. |
| 2 | Committed to regular attendance at the group, mainly for fun and friendship. |
| 1 | If there is something better elsewhere, they don't come to youth group. |
| 0 | No current youth group. |

The diocese was surveyed, and 130 Churches provided information.

The first surprise was that 24 per cent of Churches had no youth groups.

The commitment level of the average youth group member in the 99 Churches that had youth ministry was:

- Level 1: 5 per cent of Churches had a majority of members with no real commitment to either the group or to being Christ-like
- Level 2: 19 per cent had a majority of members with commitment only to the youth group for its social activities
- Level 3: 44 per cent had a majority of members with commitment to Christian ideas and a belief in God
- Level 4: 27 per cent had a majority of members with commitment to living a consistent Christian life
- Level 5: 5 per cent had a majority of members with commitment to being Christ-like.

The second important result of this research was that the disciples' groups in the survey had results that showed the majority of their members were in the Level 4 or Level 5 category. This encouraged us that we were on the right track with ministry to youth.

## One Example of a Disciples' Group

One spin-off for the Church from the disciples' groups project was the resurrection of an Anglican Church in the project trial period, 1993 and into 1994. It is no exaggeration to label the change a resurrection in the Anglican Church at West Ryde, in Sydney's gentrifying north west.

The congregation had been getting older and members were moving on to a warmer climate or to retirement villages. The congregation had reached the point where they were not even able to cope with a 'maintenance mode', much less a 'mission mode' for their Church. There was a small Sunday School and no youth group.

However, the Rector had allowed Young Life, under Glyn Henman, to use the Church hall on a Friday night. The Diocesan Youth Department was able to form an agreement between the Parish Council and Young Life New South Wales. The agreement involved the Diocesan Youth Department providing help to disciple the Christians in the Young Life group, discipling them to 'have goals and values' arising from 'wanting what God wants'.

Within six months these disciples' group members were prepared to run an evening youth service once a month, then once a fortnight. Now they run a weekly youth service that draws eighty to a hundred people. The older congregation were transformed as well. One older member had complained at the first youth service that the Communion Table had been moved without permission. Six months later she was pouring out Coke in the Narthex and was heard to say how wonderful it was to see the young people reaching out to other young people.

Why did this agreement work? The Church was prepared to let a ministry occur that entailed youth ministers entering into the context of the young people and not vice versa. In the disciples' group training the young people entered into a Christian context that recognized their 'hurting', working class experience and culture. Those being trained were encouraged and challenged to 'want God's best' and to change their goals and values to those of God. It was the young people who determined when a Christian disciples' principle had been understood and accepted. They, in effect, gave permission for the group to then move to the next item in the training. The overall ambience for the training was the desire to be trained to be leaders, therefore the principles they were being trained in would become their personal values and goals and expectations.

The point I am making is not that disciples' groups are the only answer to the Anglican Churches problem in reaching youth. Though I do believe that disciples' groups would be a useful Diocesan systemic approach in many places. The thrust of my argument is that in this post-modern age we can best help young people by challenging them, in a loving context, to develop an Identity worth 'being', because its goals are worth dying for. And to help them 'craft' a Christ-like identity involves the provision of a context that offers Christian encouragement, hope and expectations. The outcome of this ministry will be an Identity of life with God that reaches into eternity.

## *Other Models for Adolescent Christian Formation*

It is timely, at this point, to return to the task given by the title of this chapter, 'Aussie Salvation: A Vision For Anglican Youth'. Identity can be developed by many other effective models for youth ministry besides the disciples' group model. Australia is a good place to identify other effective youth ministry models because of the breadth of contexts within which young people are found, due to its size and extremes of population dispersal.

The National Anglican Youth Commission of the General Synod of the ACA carried out a survey of Youth ministry in 1994. It wanted to identify youth ministries that were working successfully throughout the country. It proposed to make this information available with the aim of fostering youth ministry in the many parishes that had no such ministry. Its findings were published in its report titled *Sign of Hope* (Smith, 1994).

The research identified two key factors that were common to the youth ministry found in every parish that had good youth ministry. These were:

1.  Each parish had one or two people with a vision and commitment to foster youth ministry.
2.  In each of those parishes at least one person with a vision for youth ministry had the ability to inspire and facilitate others with their vision.

The following factors were found in the majority of Churches that were effective in youth ministry:

1.  The Church leadership gave a priority to the development of leadership and the training and encouragement of the leaders in the youth ministry. The local Church leadership ensured that the youth leaders had clear aims and opportunities to clarify their aims, methods and results.
2.  The local Church leadership valued and publicly expressed its valuing of youth ministry.
3.  Both the local Church leaders and the youth group leaders placed a high value on the spiritual development of their young people, including 'being serious about Christian teaching and commitment'.
4.  The youth group used social activities as appropriate, especially with young teenagers.

It is not hard to see why youth ministry would be strong in those parishes that implemented the above values and principles.

The diversity among the models is of interest. Each of the following successful models incorporated the above principles to foster Christian growth in its members.

The parish of Keppel (in the Diocese of Rockhampton, Queensland), had developed a youth version of the Catechumenate. The Catechumenate fits naturally to that wing of the Anglican Church that values the inculcation of the Christian tradition into its young people. Their programme, called Kid Cat, took three years for a participant to complete. Most participants were aged between 12 and 17. This faith formation process was being assessed for suitability for other parishes, at the time of the compilation of the Youth Commission Report.

Internationally developed youth movements, such as Emmaus, have been another rich vein used by some Churches to encourage their young people towards spiritual maturity. For example, the Anglican Church in the large country town of Traralgon (population 21,000 in the Diocese of Gippsland, eastern Victoria), has used Emmaus as well as the Girls Friendly Society to help in the Christian formation of their young people.

In most big cities there is a 'Bible-belt' socio-economic group. Anglican Churches in these Bible belt areas usually have the financial resources to employ theologically aware youth ministers. These Churches also usually have a wide drawing power, including university undergraduates for their leadership. The Anglican Church at Castle Hill (in the north west of Sydney), has employed a youth minister for over 20 years. It had built outreach groups, disciples' groups and other large members groups to cater for the 500 or so young people who want to attend there. The discipling of their young people has provided them with a steady stream of youth group leaders.

All of these models of youth ministry have the potential to develop young people in whom is being formed a Christ-like Identity.

## A Mature Christian Identity

I understand that Christ-like Identity to be related to Paul's concept of *teleos*. The difference being that a Christ-like Identity is a present reality for the person, but her Christian growth is towards *teleos*. According to Paul, *teleos* is the development of the person to the end for which God has called her. Our task is to guide or teach the young person to the maturity talked of in Paul's letter to the Ephesians.

Paul's notion of Christian maturity uses terms such as 'to mature manhood, to the measure of the stature of the fullness of Christ'; 'so that we may no longer be children, tossed to and fro and carried about with every wind of doctrine'. The deceits of ideologies, movements and philosophies should not be able to raise false expectations in the heart and mind of the Christ-like adolescent.

Instead she will be able to take initiatives that are consistent with her values and clear Identity. Because she will know who she is, she will have the courage to live accordingly. One of her initiatives may involve losing what is most dear to her, which is likely to be her life. But because she has values that were worthy, they will have been worth dying for. Our Lord made clear there are things much worse that death ( Luke 12:4, 'I tell you, my friends, do not fear those who kill the body, and after that can do no more.')

## Christian Identity Development as a Paradigm in Cross-Cultural Ministry

It is not just for adolescents who belong to a Western culture, that we need to understand the place of Identity. We also need to be wise when we work with people of a different culture who have come to believe in Jesus. That is, a person who still has his former cultural Identity as well as his newer Christian Identity. The New Testament epistles were written to deal with the problem of the new Christians who still had former pagan identities from some of the great Gentile cultures. They became Christians and entered into the benefits of the Kingdom of God. However, many had not transformed their former identities with a Christ-like Identity. This is shown in the warning not to look back, but to leave behind their former futile ways.

A missionary friend, Dr Julie Waddy, brought this to mind when she spoke of the difficulty some Christians from an Aboriginal community were having with curses! Dr Waddy, who is working for the Church Mission Society at Groote Eylandt in the Northern territory, related to me the issue of fear in the thinking of Aboriginal people, both Christian and non-Christian, where she ministers.

She explained, with some caution, how part of the local Aboriginal culture contains a well-developed understanding of 'black magic', with its strong curses that many people believe can lead to sickness and ultimately death. Dr Waddy prepared me to make a leap in my understanding of the local Aboriginal culture by telling me about the two apparently healthy middle-aged women who died within two weeks of each other. The people of that community had no doubt as to black magic being the cause.

Her disturbing story concerned a prominent Aboriginal Christian leader who was hospitalized in great pain recently. The doctors carried out exploratory surgery but were unable to find any cause of his intense pain. He, however, suspected that someone had tried to do something to him. He had suspected that for a while, and though he knew in his head that God's power is stronger, his gut-level response led him to believe his cultural up-bringing which had taught him that 'when someone places a black magic curse on you, you will die – nothing can be more certain'. He and his family struggled to bring the two belief systems together and allow God's power to overrule but, in the end, his cultural expectations come true and he died an untimely death. The problem was more than a cognitive understanding problem. To me the notion of Identity will be more fruitful in considering what we are to learn from this experience than the question of the type of faith he had.

This repeatedly occurring tragedy in many cultures, raises the whole question of the development of a new Christian's Identity. How does a new Christian subsume and transform her previous cultural or religious identity, especially in the case of older adolescents and adults. Many of the New Testament epistles call on new Christians to 'Consider yourself ...', to ' be as people ...', to 'imitate me ...'. It is a Pauline imperative to be who you are! This is an Identity-type issue rather than only a cognitive faith issue.

## *Realizing the Dream of a Church that has Expectations of Developing Christ-Like Adolescents*

The paradox we face is that if we are prepared to die we will yield much fruit, but choosing to die is rarely easy. Young people need Christians to enter their world, to love them and to offer them God's context in which to develop expectations, goals and values. However, it is hard to leave our habitual contexts to enter those of young people. It may be even harder, personally, for each of us to provide Christian contexts for today's adolescents to worship God in. The Apostle Paul did it! But it was hard for the Apostle Peter to change his understanding of what the Christian community would have to change too so as to include Cornelius and the other Gentile Christians.

One sign of Christ-likeness in our adolescents will be our sense of being uncomfortable in their presence, because their expectations of this life will be, at times, more Christ-like than ours. I believe the choice the Anglican Church ultimately makes about ministry to youth will reveal the extent to which our expectations are Christ-like.

FURTHER READING

Abbott-Smith, G. *A Greek Lexicon of the New Testament* . T. & T. Clark

Aksham, J. Identity and Stability in Marriage, Cambridge University Press, 1984.

Cronbach, L. J. *Educational Psychology*, ed. Rupert Hart-Davis. 2nd edn, 1963.

Girard, in *Raising Abel: The Recovery of the Eschatological Imagination*, ed. by James Alison. Crossroad/Herder.

From THE TABLET, 29 June 1996. p 848

Kondo. D., 1990, *Crafting Selves*. The University of Chicago Press.

Smith, T. R., 1993 *Go for Godliness*. Christian Education Publications.

Smith, T. R., 1994 *Signs of Hope*. The National Anglican Youth Commission. The Commission surveyed the national Church by asking each Diocesan Youth Ministry contact or the local Bishop to select Churches where youth ministry is going well. It then identified the key factors, in the 34 parishes that were nominated, to identify the common key factors that go towards a local Church having a strong and vital youth ministry.

# 9

# Where Two Worlds Meet:
## Working with Young People in Paraguay

*Patrick Butler*

I first came to Paraguay in the heart of South America in 1989 as a volunteer with the Anglican Church. A lot of things happened during the year I was here. I became fascinated by this little known country of four million (tourists tend to by-pass Paraguay for more glamorous places); I got to know a lot of young people (once I had mastered sufficient Spanish); I experienced a military coup (after 35 years in power anyone has outstayed their welcome); and I fell in love with an English girl (or so her passport said, being the daughter of missionaries she had spent over half her life in Argentina).

When we got married on English soil a year later, Rosie and I wondered whether God might open doors for us to return to South America. But it was only when we received a letter from a Paraguayan Anglican pastor saying 'we have identified a weakness in youth ministry – we believe you would be the right people to help us', that we felt it right to return. Even then it wasn't immediate, so with one small son and five years later we found ourselves flying to Asunción, Paraguay's capital city of just over one million people.

My previous youthwork experience had taken me to the East End of London, a council estate in Hull and the leafy suburbs of Chigwell in Essex. Yet even with a professional qualification and a couple of years at Bible College thrown in, it didn't seem much preparation as we settled into the heat and humidity of this subtropical, landlocked country. The job was loosely defined as 'Diocesan Youth Coordinator', though we knew that we would have to define what this meant as we went along. As in most Latin American countries, the Anglican Church became established here on two fronts. First through its chaplaincy work with the traders at the turn of the century, and secondly through the first SAMS (South American Missionary Society) missionaries who came to work with the indigenous Indians of the Chaco. It wasn't until the 1950s that the work amongst the Spanish-speaking populations of the urban areas began.

Today 'La Iglesia Anglicana Paraguaya' consists of five congregations in Asunción, one in Concepción (some 300 miles to the north) and, across the river in the vast swampy expanse of land that makes up half the country known as the Chaco, numerous indigenous Indian Churches. It is also responsible for two schools in Asunción: Colegio San Andrés (St. Andrew's College) which educates children from some of Paraguay's wealthiest families, and the Annexe School which provides for children from the Chacarita shanty town that lies along the banks of the River Paraguay. It is a small Church numerically, but extraordinarily diverse and described by Samuel Escobar as 'The only non Catholic Church that is effectively evangelizing all levels of society'.[1]

At the time of our arrival the Anglican Church was in a time of transition – longing to move from foreign to national leadership yet struggling to see mature leaders emerge. The city congregations were seeing very little growth and we found that this reflected the situation facing all Protestant denominations in Paraguay. Even the Pentecostals, who have seen rapid expansion in other Latin countries, are much smaller here. The Catholic Church, dominating the spiritual and political life of the nation, only sees a small percentage of the population in Mass and, as Patrick Johnstone observes, 'Paraguay has never had a true awakening'.[2] So it was clear to us that youth ministry in this climate would present it's challenges, but we hoped to be able to work alongside our Paraguayan colleagues in seeing Christ proclaimed amongst young people here.

Almost four years later, our work has put us into contact (and often close contact) with young people from almost every strata of Paraguayan society. Anybody who has worked in a cross-cultural situation will testify to the time it takes to adjust to a new culture and a lot of lessons have been learned along the way. So in the following pages I aim to share some of the ways our experiences we have affected our youthwork practise. But first, in order to put these observations into context, let me outline what I identify as 10 characteristics of Paraguayan youth culture.

### 1. YOUNG PEOPLE ARE IN THE MAJORITY

South America is a continent of youth and in Paraguay 62 per cent of the population are under 24 years old. In the *barrios* young people play volleyball with nets strung across the earth roads, while others hang around the newly constructed shopping malls. The rich kids cruise around in their 4x4's while the street kids jump on and off buses selling anything they can, from watches to chewing gum to nail clippers. In Paraguay no one can afford to be unemployed. Young people are growing up in a rapidly changing society and businesses invest millions in advertising aimed at the young, whilst an under-funded education system tries to respond to their more basic needs.

### 2. YOUNG PEOPLE ARE BILINGUAL

In Paraguay most young people grow up speaking two languages – Guarani and Spanish, the former being the Indian 'language of the people' and the latter the language of the media, business and education. People in the countryside speak less Spanish and are most comfortable in Guarani whereas the reverse is true for the middle and upper classes in Asunción. It is usual however to hear people switch languages in mid-sentence and sometimes young people I know will be conversing in Spanish, then suddenly tell a joke in Guarani and fall about laughing. 'Sorry Patrick,' they say, knowing I can't understand, 'it just sounds so much funnier in Guarani!' It's then you realize the extent to which Guarani is the heart language and that the country is unique amongst its Latin counterparts in having maintained its Indian identity in the face of the Spanish *conquistadores*. Meanwhile across the river in the Chaco the indigenous Indian young people will very often speak Spanish and Guarani on top of their mother tongue.

### 3. YOUNG PEOPLE LOOK TO THE WEST

'*Mb'ai chapa*' reads the sticker with a big golden M on a red background. This means 'How are you?' in Guarani and also means that McDonald's has arrived. Nearly every aspect of life in Paraguay is touched by western culture, bringing with it rapid social change. In the last four years Paraguay has seen the arrival of the Internet, Burger King, Pizza Hut, Cable TV, mobile phones and shopping malls.

For young people the heroes are from the West. Rosie is currently marking project work for her class of 14-year-olds to whom she teaches English. Among them are essays on Michael Jackson, Leonardo di Caprio, The Beatles and Oasis. The queues to see *Titanic* lasted weeks and Nike, Reebok, Levis and Benetton are in the clothes shops and, in varying qualities of fake, on the streets. Turn on the radio and alongside the Brazilian Sambas and Argentine Rock will be the English and US rock groups and, on national TV, *Baywatch* and *Beverly Hills 90210*.

At Colegio San Andrés the majority of pupils are dropped off at school by their chauffeurs. Their houses have maids and their gardens swimming pools. Their weekends are spent in country clubs and they holiday in Miami. 'Other kids call us "San Anjet",' Maria tells me, commenting on the prejudice from other colleges. 'But when they get to know us they really like us.'

These young people live in two worlds – physically in Paraguay, yet culturally looking to the West. Paraguayan journalist José Zanardini comments on this 'cultural schizophrenia' he perceives in Paraguay's wealthy youth.

> These young people who paint the walls of Asunción announcing their fabulous parties; these young people with no limits to the number of beer cans they empty; these young people who despise their country of origin; these young people who are politically and socially hollow; these young people who have huge economic means at their disposal – they are victims of an alienating cultural imperialism and social complexity they themselves did not create. We are witnessing a cultural disassociation between the country within which they live and the country in which they would like to live and the effects of globalization on these young people are disasterous.[3]

Meanwhile Cesar offers me a lift across town in his father's Mercedes. It doesn't seem to bother him (or his father) that he is only 15 and doesn't have a driving licence, and like many of his contemporaries he is looking forward to the day when he can study and work overseas. 'There are so many more opportunities abroad' he says, 'though I'm sure I would return to Paraguay.' But many don't, and after exposure to elsewhere see little that is good about their country.

### 4. YOUNG PEOPLE FEEL INFERIOR

There is a lack of self-confidence in many young people, with a strong sense that they belong to an inferior nation.

At the youth camp Miguel, José and Mario were planning a sketch to perform around the bonfire. It was a variation of the 'Englishman, Irishman, Scotsman' joke (every nation has them – where one nationality ends up doing something daft), in this case a Chilean an Argentine and a Paraguayan. When I saw the finished result it took me a moment to register that they had chosen to make their own country the butt of the joke!

Time and again you see this sense of inferiority amongst young people. 'Do you like it living here?' Rocio asks me. 'Honestly?' she says, not believing I could possibly answer yes. They know they are in an underdeveloped nation where corruption is woven into the fabric; where politicians line their own bank accounts with impunity whilst investment in health and education remain at a minimum; they know that they are considered 'backward' by their more powerful and influential Brazilian and Argentine neighbours.

The Guarani expression '*Opa re*' is often used here. It means that nothing is ever carried through to its proper conclusion and the expectation is that things will inevitably fail. This self-defeatism is then used as an excuse for poor planning which re-enforces the poor self-image: 'What else do you expect from Paraguay.' Though they may be happy to put themselves down, there exists, however, a fierce national pride and sensitivity towards criticism from outsiders. The press will report at great length anything written about the country in the foreign media. But the cries of the football commentator when Paraguay beat Nigeria in the World Cup of 'you see we're not an inferior nation', shows the extent to which they believe they are. These deep seated feelings are huge obstacles for a new generation to overcome.

## 5. YOUNG PEOPLE AREN'T 'HARD'

When you come from a culture where anyone in contact with teenagers will field at least some abuse, the contrast here is striking. There is a refreshing absence of sarcasm and the need to 'put down', and even young people from the poorest *barrios* will meet you half way without having to prove how 'hard' they are. When you meet someone you know and who is with a group of friends, you shake hands with each person individually and give a kiss to anyone of the opposite sex. The casual nod that passes for a greeting in England is woefully inadequate. The culture here demands that you are recognized and acknowledged as a human being. Even drinking the national tea – tereré – is a social occasion as the *guampa* is passed round to each person in turn, who sucks from a metal straw.

Walking past a group of teenagers on the streets of Asunción I don't experience the same unease as in the UK. There, I am not certain of escaping without some comment (or even object) being thrown my way. Here, if I say *'hola'* as I go by, I will very likely get a polite *'hola'* in return (though a girl can expect a comment or two). It seems that people generally are accepted for who they are. At school the other day an obviously handicapped boy was lead across the playground to the staff room. I was all set for the inevitable embarrassed giggles from the students, but even though they saw him, they carried on with their conversations without any anonymous shouts of 'spazzy'.

There is considerable crime in Paraguay and in the 10 years since the end of the dictatorship it has risen markedly. Nearly all houses have bars on the windows, armed security guards are everywhere and twice I have seen 'crazy horses' grab jewellery or handbags and run from the buses. There is also trafficking of everything from drugs (though relatively little consumption) and babies, to cars – 80 per cent of which are without legal documents! Yet 'anti-social' behaviour such as football violence or vandalism simply isn't here. If something is broken or out of order it is more likely to be due to a violent storm or poor workmanship than bored young people. The little park just down our road recently had free floodlighting installed for 5-aside football and basketball. This was done under the Council's much publicised scheme to promote sports throughout the city. As there was no one apparently controlling the use of this facility I wasn't surprised to find that, after a couple of weeks the lights weren't working. 'Vandalism?' I asked the lady at the café. 'No' , she replied, 'the Council never paid the electricity bill!'

## 6. YOUNG PEOPLE BELIEVE IN GOD

Whereas the UK is an essentially secular culture, Paraguay is fundamentally religious, with strong respect for the Catholic Church. So on the buses passengers cross themselves as they pass a Church, footballers cross themselves as they go onto the pitch and pictures of the virgin Mary hang happily next to photos of topless pin-up girls in garages and offices.

The question, 'Do you believe in God?' might be a point for debate in Europe, but is not relevant here as very few seem to hold an agnostic or atheist standpoint. Of the young people we talked to in a street survey in the centre of Asunción almost all (and most were very happy to stop and talk) said they believed in God and would call themselves Christians. Yet their uncertainty at the question, 'What do you think will happen to you when you die?' showed they were uncertain as to the basis of their faith. It is also clear that belief has little influence over behaviour, and faith in God is entirely compatible with accepting bribes, having an extra-marital affair or cheating in an exam.

In his classic *The Other Spanish Christ*, written at the turn of the century, John A. Mackay gives a fascinating account of the arrival of the Catholic Church in South America. Although people appeared to convert to Catholicism, 'the heart was not changed and the mind was not enlightened', and he goes on to say that the Christ the *conquistadores* brought with them was not the Christ of the Scriptures, rather:

> A Christ who was not born in Bethlehem but in North Africa, a Christ who became naturalised in the Iberian colonies of America, while Mary's son and Lord has been little else than a stranger and a sojourner in these lands from Columbus's day to this.[4]

Though much has changed since then and there are Catholic Churches who preach a clear Gospel, for most of the population faith in God boils down to little more than a superstitious folk religion. Young people seem to have no problem in rising to their feet at the appeal of a visiting Protestant evangelist, but it will very likely be a superficial response that has little to do with a lasting commitment to Christ.

## 7. YOUNG PEOPLE ARE CONSERVATIVE

Compared to Europe where youth movements emerge periodically to shock the adult generation (the Teddy Boys of the '50s, Punks in the '70s, Rave culture of the '90s), Paraguayan young people are pushing very few boundaries. They tend to be conventional in dress (stylish maybe, but not alternative), and though the wealthy attend parties and nightclubs, any 'alternative culture' that may exist keeps a low profile. This conservatism is reflected in other ways too where few young people seem to demonstrate a concern and passion for wider issues such as politics, ecology or human rights.

In some ways this is inevitable in a small country with few resources, but three other factors play a part. One is an education system that emphasizes learning by rote and repetition, thus discouraging creativity and free thinking. Schools have few books and resources and teachers are often poorly trained. At university level, where most students study part-time, there is little time for reflection through essays, more an emphasis on absorbing facts and figures.

A second is the legacy of the dictatorship where Alfredo Stroessner ruled Paraguay for 35 years, crushing virtually all opposition, until he was ousted in a military coup in 1989. This means that people have inherited a tradition of submission and silence, and still think twice about standing out from the crowd and raising their voices. So it was significant in April 1996 when, for the first time in Paraguay's recent history, students came out onto the streets in protest against an attempted coup which would have put a military general in power once more. Their action in support of democracy helped to bring about a peaceful end to the crisis.

A third factor is the way that young people are under pressure to conform by a previous generation. Leaders tend to be authoritarian and will often 'lower the cane' to bring the next generation into line. This may be done through direct confrontation but more often through rumour and social pressure, which proves to be a very effective way of making people conform.

### 8. YOUNG PEOPLE BELONG TO A FAMILY

The extended family here plays a significant role in society. Children grow up surrounded by grandparents, aunts and uncles and spend a lot of time with their cousins who are often their best friends. So young people grow up with a sense of identity and belonging that in many cases has been lost in the UK.

With no Welfare State the family becomes crucial as the main provider of care for the old and infirm and, in a society where abortion is illegal, absorbing the large number of children born out of wedlock. Though divorce was illegal until recently, the nuclear family is often a disaster with either an absent father or children by several fathers. Whereas the freedom of the 1960s and the discovery of the Pill paved the way for the sexual revolution in the UK, here sexual behaviour is more formed by a tradition where men have mistresses as well as wives. Apart from that, two disastrous wars (in 1860 and 1932), through which the country lost 80 per cent of its male population, meant that a degree of sexual freedom was required in order for the country to repopulate itself.

In some cases 'unwanted' pregnancies are even encouraged. The lady at our local corner shop was thrilled her daughter was providing her with a grandchild and didn't mind in the least that she wasn't in a stable relationship! Far more serious would have been for her daughter to have been left a childless 'old maid'!

### 9. YOUNG PEOPLE HAVE LITTLE TIME

Selina is 19 years old and she gets up at 5.30 a.m. every morning. From her home in the outskirts of Asunción she takes a bus to the city centre where she starts her day's work as a secretary at 7.30 a.m. As soon as she finishes at 4 p.m. she takes another bus across town to the university where she is studying accountancy. When classes end at 7.30 p.m. she has a bite to eat with some friends before taking the bus back home, arriving around 9 p.m. On Saturdays she cleans the house, does the washing and spends time with her mentally ill father, who Selina's sister (a single parent) looks after during the week. Their mother died a year ago. On Saturday evenings Selina attends the Church youth group and on Sundays, after the morning service, she does some study and rests.

Selina is typical of many young people who, with pressures of work, study and family responsibilities have very little free time indeed. So much time is spent simply buying food and medicines, getting things repaired and paying bills. Many young people can't afford to finish their education and must find work – no matter how menial, and those who are fortunate to study at university do so in the evenings, working during the day to pay for the fees. In the summer months when the heat and humidity is at its highest, the routine is relentless and exhausting.

## 10. YOUNG PEOPLE ARE POORLY RESOURCED

As might be expected the myriad of clubs, camps, outward bound centres, leisure facilities, books, magazines, educational tools and support networks available to young people in developed countries simply are not here. Though the government has a 'Secretary for Youth' there is no Youth Service as such, and a struggling Social Service directs all its attention to the multiple needs of crisis young people. So most work with young people outside schools is done by Churches and organizations such as the Scouts and the YMCA, using what resources they have.

As far as leisure is concerned, those with money join sports clubs for swimming and tennis and go to the cinema, while those without will settle for TV and a game of football in the *barrio*. On a Sunday afternoon you will find many young letting off steam in a game of volleyball before sitting around with cans of beer whilst listening to *cachaca* – a sort of Latin reggae with melancholy lyrics and best played at full volume.

## Negotiating the Obstacles

When we first arrived in Paraguay we were keen, as mission partners, for our role to be one of training and resourcing rather than doing. We believed we could best develop the youth work of the Church by training the older young people who had remained faithful to their congregations in youth leadership. With our support they could then take the work forward. But working with the above cultural factors wasn't so easy, and as we progressed we found an impressive range of obstacles in our way.

To begin with we had underestimated the time it would take to 'earn the right' and gain people's confidence. Once we got beyond the initial friendly contact with young people we discovered just how different they were, and building deep relationships was long term and hard work. It was important too to simply spend time with people and we found the most valuable visits were the spontaneous ones, where we would sit round drinking tereré and talking about nothing in particular.

We had not appreciated the extent to which improvization is a part of the culture and the reasons for this. Youth meetings and events would be thrown together at the last minute and either somehow worked or didn't. But with young people being so busy it was hard to meet for the necessary prior planning and when we finally did arrange a time together, either a torrential storm or a bus strike would put us back to square one. With few on the phone (the whole of Paraguay fits into one directory!), it could take a whole afternoon just to set up another meeting.

One of the most important lessons we learned was the influence of the family. As with many Churches, the Anglican Church here is clan orientated, with almost all the pastors and a large number of the congregation related to each other. We found that with the youth activities we planned, if the young people didn't sense that the family were in support of what was happening, no one would turn up on the day. Likewise if we gave responsibility to a person who did not enjoy the tacit approval of the family, his or her sphere of influence would be remarkably limited!

Theologically we encountered a super-spirituality that refused to engage with the surrounding youth culture, drawing a clear distinction between the Church and 'the world'. Many young people, well versed in religious language but tired of black and white answers that did not speak to their reality, would spend years leading a double life before eventually rejecting the Church altogether.

On a practical level the lack of funds and resources available made it hard to plan anything that involved travelling or equipment (in the end we had to rely on a degree of foreign funding to subsidize camps and visits), and lastly, the very job we were doing caused confusion in a country where full-time youthworkers, either

Christian or secular, don't exist. 'So you're not a pastor then?' people would ask. 'Yes, but what's your *real* job?' One of the best moves in our third year was to begin teaching in Colegio San Andrés – itself a key area for youth ministry – which gave us a 'real job' whilst enabling us to continue supporting the Churches in their youth ministry.

One of my greatest learning points, however, came after two years here and involved the youth group at the Cathedral. Javier and Victor, both in their twenties, had taken responsibility for leading the group but, for various reasons, had stepped down leaving no one else to fill the void but me. Having found it frustrating that the programme had never been planned more than a week in advance, I decided that at the first meeting we would draw up a programme for the term together. I gave each member (around a dozen) a piece of paper each and got them to write down five things they enjoyed doing, and three things they wanted to learn about.

We then wrote the results up on a board and from this started to develop a programme of activities and teaching. The atmosphere was great and the group participated enthusiastically. What we came out with was a fun and varied programme looking at the things they wanted to learn about and doing the things they wanted to do. What was even better was that various members were willing to take charge of the different events, leaving my role as more of a facilitator which was exactly what I wanted. In terms of youthwork practise I left the meeting very pleased with how it had gone. I had not imposed and together we had come up with something involving their participation and leadership. So it was a great shock when, within two weeks, the group had all but folded! True it was quite a new group and not all that solid to start with; true exams weren't far away. But I was mystified. Here was this great programme *they* had supposedly wanted and now there was no interest whatsoever. What had happened?

Perhaps they felt uncomfortable *not* being told what to do. A strong, authoritarian leader is one who commands respect in this culture and my way of leading (though great back home) was too vague for them. Secondly, at the end of the day the implementation of the programme was down to them and they didn't feel confident enough to take the risk – or to say so. (In a 'people culture' the mood of the moment is more important than keeping your word, so a 'yes, we'll be there' may be sincerely meant but not to be depended upon!) Thirdly, Javier and Victor had been a part of 'the family' and the group had felt safe with that. Finally, in a culture where youth meetings tend simply to mirror what happens in the Sunday services, what we had on the board was simply too ambitious. Whatever – all I was left with was one great learning experience!!

### Things that work

So, obstacles and lessons learned aside, what *has* worked in Anglican youth ministry in Paraguay? I can point to several things that have been achieved and can be built on over the next few years.

The first is the development of the *twice yearly diocesan camps*. Using a site belonging to another Church, with basic but adequate cabins and set in a beautiful part of the countryside with a stream for swimming, we have held five of these – drawing together around 60 young people from the different congregations. The weekends are well structured, combining biblical teaching on relevant themes with workshops, sports and exploration. Young people gain experience in leading the different aspects of the camp and the pastors often come too, which we have found has built a better trust and understanding with their young people. The camps have also gone a long way to building the pastors' confidence in us, particularly when we have explored elements of youth culture – thus showing that we can be a resource in their attempts to come to grips with the rapidly changing realities of the next generation.

Secondly, we are able to *serve as a bridge* for this next generation as they struggle to reconcile the faith of their parents with the world around them. Coming from the very culture that is making such an impact on their lives, we are able to point to biblical principles that lead to discernment, rather than rejecting the culture as a whole. They sense that in our company (and this hasn't been achieved overnight) they have the space to express doubts and confusion without being judged. Some, like Ruth, have worked things through to a clear and reasoned faith; others, like Danilo, pop round from time to time to listen to Beatles tapes and tell me about his band. At the moment he has nothing to do with the Church, but I am glad to be one of the few remaining links.

A third contribution made has been in the area of *music in worship*. Most Churches have a music group and these are usually led by young people. *Guarani* and Latin songs are sung less and less, in favour of choruses translated from Britain and the States and though I (as a musician) would love them to use what is part of their own culture, like it or not the West is considered best, and the most practical thing I can do is help them to play it well. So I have invested time teaching young people guitar and bass and this has given them much more confidence in expressing themselves through this musical style.

But Paraguay is far from the 'alternative worship' that has been developed in the UK over the past 10 years. Here the first Paraguayan Christian rock bands are only just emerging (with names such as 'Pax', 'Sanctus' and 'Judah'), and are still viewed with suspicion by many leaders who find their basic heavy rock yet solid evangelical theology impossible to reconcile. But for Christian young people in their teens and twenties they are a vital bridge to survival, providing them with at least something they can participate in that connects with the surrounding culture.

We have also been able to use music as a bridge with the young indigenous Indians of the Chaco. Every year they hold a music festival there to which we bring young people from the city to participate in. Amidst the wooden huts with no electricity, where these hunter gatherer people cook on open fires, the young people, of the same nationality but from vastly different worlds, find a common denominator through music and more of an awareness of the others' reality.

Likewise, participating in bi-annual *Provincial camps* with Anglican young people of the Southern Cone has had a tremendous impact on the Paraguayan young people. Through these they have gained a greater sense of identity and belonging to the Anglican Communion as they have built friendships and established support networks with their Latin brothers and sisters in Christ. At the last camp in Argentina it was significant to hear the group of six that attended laughing together in *Guarani* and saying 'we feel so good here being Paraguayans'. The experience did a lot for their self-esteem. The next camp will be in Peru in 2000.

A fourth area of work has been the production of a *basic training manual* for youth leadership. This was commissioned by the Province, realizing that much of the youth ministry material coming over from the States, failed to speak to our reality as

Anglicans of the Southern Cone. Co-written by myself, an Argentine and a Chilean youthworker, we have made it as practical as possible, aiming at younger potential leaders who may be facing the challenge of youthwork in small Churches. It's a resource we will be promoting in the Southern Cone over the next two years.

Fifthly we have found our work in *Colegio San Andrés* an exciting area of youth ministry. Through the school, God has given the Anglican Church a unique opportunity to reach some of the most influential families in Paraguay with the Gospel. We have been able to develop some close relationships with students, start various after-school activities (including a prayer group) and also lay plans to launch a major initiative called EJE.

*Encuentro Juvenil en el Espiritu (EJE)* or 'Youth Encounter in the Spirit', grew out of the Catholic Church and was taken and adapted by the Anglican Church in Chile around five years ago. Since then it has had a tremendous impact on young people (Christian and non Christian) in both Chile and Argentina, and has been a tremendous stimulus to the Churches' work with young people. EJE centres around an encounter weekend, which focuses on relationships and to which young people can only attend if invited by a friend who has already done EJE. It is something entirely Latin and many young people come to a commitment to Christ through the experience. Establishing EJE in Paraguay will be a long-term initiative and something, we pray, will affect not only the Anglican youth work but those of other denominations too.

Lastly, we have had the privilege of *accompanying a few* into mature faith and youth leadership. We have seen relatively few leaders emerge from the congregations but, over the past four years, God has given us some close friendships. There is one young couple we have spent a lot of time with and as well as meeting regularly for Bible study and later marriage preparation. They are currently meeting with a group of young people in their home and expecting their first child. I know we are as much an encouragement to them as they are to us.

### Returning to the first world

There is alot of truth in the old saying: 'missionaries usually overestimate what can be achieved in two years and underestimate what can be achieved in ten', and we are just beginning to see green shoots emerge where a year ago the ground seemed barren. At several points we almost gave up, feeling too 'foreign' and wondering what more we could contribute, but now we can see clear patterns for youth ministry emerging.

As I write this we are preparing for our first visit to the UK in almost four years. There will be some catching up to do when the plane lands, though a lot of what is news there is already news here. Paraguayan young people know in great detail about the death of Diana and the demise of the Spice Girls, whereas UK children will be lucky to place Paraguay in the correct continent. Such is the one-sidedness of 'globalization'; it is here where the two worlds collide and young people feel the impact of that collision.

Youth ministry is tough wherever you are, each place bringing its own challenges and obstacles. Here, a tragic history, rapid social change, a disastrous economy and an unstable political scene creates a particularly challenging backdrop for this part of the body of Christ in its outreach to young people in Paraguay. So we are taking a short break in the 'other world', but look forward to continuing our work alongside the Anglican Church as it seeks to build the Kingdom of God in this one.

## Notes

1. *South American Missionary Society Journal*: 'The elephant and the Ant'
2. Patrick Johnstone OM, *Operation World*, 1993, p.442.
3. Resistencia Cultural Juvenil. *Ultima Hora* 25 and 26 October 1996.
4. David A. Mackay, *The Other Spanish Christ*, SCM Press p.95.

# Postscript

## The Lambeth Conference and 'A Youthful Spirit'

### *Lindsay Urwin OGS and David Moxon*

In his presidential address at the beginning of the 1998 Lambeth Conference, the Archbishop of Canterbury placed a strong emphasis on encouraging the Communion in the work of renewal and mission. He stressed the importance of the 'local' in effective evangelization, and affirmed and encouraged the Provinces to express worship and faith in ways which make connections with their own culture.

We are well used to speaking of the African, Asian or South American culture and in many communities actively encourage and delight in the diversity of those who make up what Desmond Tutu delightfully describes as the 'rainbow people of God'. No one who shared in the daily pattern of eucharist and evening worship at the Conference can have failed to marvel at the rich, even intriguing way various provinces led us in the liturgy as they locally express it.

Within this cultural mix there is also youth culture, which needs to be honoured and valued, and in the discussions of the section of the Conference devoted to mission and evangelism, and within the small group charged with making a presentation about youth ministry to a plenary session of the Conference, we were refreshed and challenged by the sheer vitality and diversity of young people and in their contribution to the life and witness of Anglicanism, whether it be as leaders in music ministry and worship in Paraguay, or as evangelists in the diocese of Mt Kilimanjaro, or as part of the synodical process in South East Asia.

During the plenary presentation, participants experienced the giftedness of young people from a multi-ethnic parish in London's East End. This dynamic group exhausted the gathering with the acrobatics and cheerleading. Led by the American-born wife of the parish priest, through their involvement in the group the young people not only learn skills and teambuilding, but also express their commitment by going out in the local community visiting and caring for older people. A small group drawn together for the Conference wrote and performed a dramatic presentation which drew together the tragic story of Dunblane in Scotland, which saw the massacre of a group of children from a primary school, and the biblical story of the feeding of the five thousand. Youth leaders from the Holy Land and the Philippines shared their experiences, as did five bishops.

As never before, young people are the 'connected generation', who through media and globally distributed entertainment, multinational corporations and mass communications, are more aware of each other, and in the midst of world wide ethnic variety, aspire not only to Western material values, but to be heard and participate in the formation of change in the life of our planet, and indeed, the life of the Church.

A video presentation during the plenary session, allowed young people from all over the Communion to speak to the bishops gathered in Canterbury. They testified to blessings received from their belonging to the Church, but also challenged the bishops to listen more to the voices of young people and address the pressing problems of our day, among them drugs, poverty, debt and materialism. More than aware of the many voices and attractions offering alternatives to the Christian message, they call upon the bishops to help in focusing more energy in evangelizing the unconnected young.

This call is reflected in a number of specific challenges made at the end of the plenary session. That they echoed the resolutions prepared by the section and passed by the Conference encourages us to believe that they are timely and of the Lord. Specifically directed to the bishops, they have a wider application of course, and we pray that they will encourage a new wave of ministry with and among the young people of our world:

- We give thanks to God for the many young baptised believers throughout the world and especially those in our Anglican Communion.

- We salute those who encourage them in their faith and apostolic witness, and we salute young people themselves who in the midst of the many voices calling them to follow have responded to the call of Jesus and are seeking to live this way.

- Brothers and sisters, those of us who have been called to walk in the footsteps of the apostles have a particular responsibility to nurture the young.

- Our Lord warned the first apostles not to hinder the young from finding a place in his arms, so we must look to our own lives, and the style of our ministry to ensure that we are not guilty of such a grievous fault.

- Young people are attracted by lives of dedicated service, authentic holiness. In the western world with its cynicism about institutions we have a particular responsibility to minimize unnecessary bureaucracy and any inappropriate expressions of hierarchy which hinder the Church's vocation to reflect the service and humility of the Lord.

- In other parts of the Communion resources are few, and communications difficult, but there is more vibrancy and intimacy and more respect between young and old, but still bishops can seem remote and distant.

- We know the best evangelists of young people are likely to be other young people, yet there is an important place for the bishop in encouraging their Christian life and as a teacher of faith.

- The Holy Spirit is forever young. For those who live in the life of the Spirit age need be no barrier to communication. The day of Pentecost transformed the possibilities for human relationships.

- Brothers and sisters, Pray that God will grant you a youthfulness of spirit. Trust that generational and cultural difference is not a barrier in your own relationship with the young people in your diocese.

- We challenge you to meet with young people in your diocese. Although you may have priests or laity who work on your behalf with young people, we believe that it is likely that the structures seem to young people to separate you from them.

- Specifically we ask you to return to your diocese resolved to meet personally with a group of young people to listen to them, to ask them about their hopes and vision and the way they understand the world, to pray with them, to open the scriptures with them, to break bread within six months of this conference, and that should become a regular part of your ministry.

- Such a resolution is a small beginning and yet if you respond it would mean that across the globe some tens of thousands of young people would be in direct touch with their bishops. It will involve a reorientating of your time and priorities. If you are too busy to meet with your young people, then brothers and sisters, you are indeed too busy.
- Your meetings should work towards a plan of action which allows young people to minister in appropriate ways, to participate in worship and contribute to the proclamation of Christ and to social action. It should also include the development of a voice of young people in the consultative process which leads to decision making in your diocese.
- We also suggest a network of people throughout the Communion committed to assisting bishops and others as they seek to understand and speak to the young people and their culture.
- The gift of episcopal ordination brings us many joys and weighty responsibilities. We believe that a renewed emphasis on our ministry with young people will enrich our lives, and theirs, and it is vital to the development of a world which better reflects the values of God's kingdom.

The Archbishop's address spoke of the dangers of loveless evangelism, when he quoted the Welsh poet R.S. Thomas: 'They listened to one preaching the unique Gospel of love, but our eyes never met.'

May the God-given eyes of the bishops meet with the God-given eyes of the young people! In such a meeting we shall surely be given a new vision for our life together, and in the strength of the ever youthful Spirit, be given the energy to proclaim the Gospel afresh in our generation.